THE BEAN TREES

NOTES

including
- *Life and Background of the Author*
- *Introduction to the Novel*
- *A Brief Synopsis*
- *List of Characters*
- *Critical Commentaries*
- *Map*
- *Critical Essays*
- *Review Questions and Essay Topics*
- *Kingsolver's Published Works*
- *Selected Bibliography*

by
Suzanne Pavlos, M.Ed.
Stephen F. Austin State University
Nacogdoches, Texas

D1194959

INCORPORATED

LINCOLN, NEBRASKA 68501

Editor	Senior Project Editor
Gary Carey, M.A. *University of Colorado*	*Pamela Mourouzis*
Editor	Copy Editor
Greg Tubach	*Kathleen Dobie*

ISBN 0-7645-8508-8
© Copyright 1999
by
Cliffs Notes, Inc.
All Rights Reserved
Printed in U.S.A.

1999 Printing

Library of Congress
Catalog Card No.: 99-64190

Cliffs Notes, Inc.   Lincoln, Nebraska

CONTENTS

Center Spread: Taylor's Route to Tuscon, Arizona

THE BEAN TREES
Notes

LIFE AND BACKGROUND OF THE AUTHOR

Barbara Kingsolver is a contemporary American author of best-selling novels, non-fiction, and poetry. She is also a freelance journalist and political activist. Because she cares deeply about the world in which she lives and the people in it, her writing is her attempt to change the world—to make the world a better place to live. Kingsolver writes about current social issues such as the environment, human rights, and injustice. The protagonists in her writing portray resilient, sensitive females successfully surviving typical day-to-day struggles. Although Kingsolver writes about serious subjects and her characters face traumatic dilemmas, she is also able to interject humor, which lightens the tone and communicates the love, hope, and strength evident in the lives of people from all cultures and walks of life. Her personal experiences and passions, as well as the environment of the southwestern United States, influence her writing.

Kingsolver was born on April 8, 1955, in Annapolis, Maryland, to Wendell Kingsolver, a physician, and Virginia Henry. Her family soon moved to be close to relatives living in eastern Kentucky. Kingsolver's father worked as the only doctor in rural Nicholas County, a county situated between the poverty of coal fields and the affluence of horse farms. Nicholas County was an economically depressed area, and most people living there were not well off; they earned only enough money to ensure their survival through tobacco farming. Nicholas County did not have a swimming pool, and Kingsolver never laid eyes on a tennis court until she went away to college.

From an early age, Kingsolver enjoyed telling stories (her parents *listened* to bedtime stories instead of telling them). And because her parents were intolerant of television, Kingsolver spent her time reading and writing stories and essays. Living in the country amid fields and woods, Kingsolver became a student of nature.

Plants and animals fascinated her and often found their way into her parents' house. Her parents were generally understanding; however, they did not allow snakes and mice inside.

In 1962, Kingsolver's father chose to practice medicine where he felt he could make a significant difference in the lives of others. He took his family first to St. Lucia, an island nation in the Caribbean, where they lived in a convent hospital, and then to central Africa. While living in Africa, Kingsolver experienced what it was like to be a minority and an outsider. She was the only white child in the village. At the time, her hair was long enough to sit on, and the village children, never having seen hair like Kingsolver's, tried to pull it off as though it were some sort of headpiece. Kingsolver's experiences opened her eyes to the world and provoked her curiosity about people from other cultures. By the time she was eight years old, Kingsolver resolutely kept a daily journal and entered every essay contest for which she was eligible.

Other important influences on Kingsolver during her childhood included the county Bookmobile, large family vegetable gardens, and a community that depended on the kindness of others to get by.

Having returned to Nicholas County to attend public school, Kingsolver graduated from Nicholas County High School in 1973. She then attended DePauw University in Greencastle, Indiana, on a scholarship to study instrumental music, a lifelong interest of hers. In college, Kingsolver changed her major to biology and worked to eliminate her rural Kentucky accent and the expressions she had adopted from that particular region, both of which seemed to invite teasing. (Much later, Kingsolver realized how unique her language was and has attempted to re-create it in her writing.) While in college, she was exposed to the writings of feminist authors Betty Friedan and Gloria Steinem and studied German philosophers and socialists Karl Marx and Friedrich Engels. She took one creative writing class and participated in anti-Vietnam War protests. She graduated from DePauw magna cum laude in 1977 with a Bachelor of Arts degree and then moved to Tucson, Arizona, where she began graduate studies in biology and ecology at the University of Arizona and worked as a research assistant in the physiology department until 1979.

After receiving a Master of Science degree in 1981 from the University of Arizona, Kingsolver accepted a job at the university and began writing science articles. She also pursued additional graduate studies and took a writing class with author Francine Prose. It was then that she realized that she did not want to pursue a career in academia but, rather, wanted to write. She began working as a freelance scientific writer and journalist. Her articles have appeared in *The Progressive, Smithsonian Magazine,* and *The Sonoran Review.* Kingsolver also began writing short stories that have been published in *Redbook, Mademoiselle,* and anthologies such as *New Stories from the South: The Year's Best, 1988; Florilegia, an Anthology of Art and Literature by Women;* and *Rebirth of Power.*

Kingsolver began a nonfiction book in 1983 about the copper mine strike against the Phelps Dodge Corporation in Arizona. She spent hours interviewing union wives about their experiences during and after the strike. A year later, the book was only half finished, and because her agent was having trouble selling it, Kingsolver stopped working on the book and returned to freelance writing.

On April 15, 1985, Kingsolver married University of Arizona chemistry professor Joseph Hoffmann. She soon found herself pregnant and unable to sleep at night. Her doctor suggested that she scrub bathroom tiles with a toothbrush to battle her insomnia, but instead she sat in a closet and began writing her first novel, *The Bean Trees.* If her daughter, Camille, had not been born three weeks late, Kingsolver might never have finished *The Bean Trees,* published in 1988.

Supporting herself with the advance money from *The Bean Trees,* Kingsolver completed writing her nonfiction account of the Arizona mining strike. Published in 1989 by Cornell University Press, the work is titled *Holding the Line: Women in the Great Arizona Mine Strike of 1983.* In 1989, she also published a collection of short stories, *Homeland and Other Stories.* She then went on to write the novels *Animal Dreams* (1990) and *Pigs in Heaven* (1993), a sequel to *The Bean Trees;* a best-selling collection of poetry, *Another America: Otra America* (1992); a collection of essays, *High Tide in Tucson: Essays From Now and Never* (1995); and another novel, *The Poisonwood Bible* (1998).

Kingsolver's writing has received much acclaim. Her awards and honors include American Library Association awards for *The Bean Trees* in 1988 and *Homeland* in 1990; a citation of accomplishment from United Nations National Council of Women in 1989; a PEN fiction prize and Edward Abbey Ecofiction award, both in 1991, for *Animal Dreams*; a *Los Angeles Times* Book Award for Fiction in 1993 for *Pigs in Heaven*; and a feature-writing award from the Arizona Press Club (1996). *The Bean Trees* has been published in more than 65 countries throughout the world and was released in 1998 in a mass-market edition. In 1995, Kingsolver was awarded an Honorary Doctorate of Letters degree from her alma mater, DePauw University.

Kingsolver was divorced from her first husband in 1993. In 1995, she married Steven Hopp, an ornithologist, animal behaviorist, and guitarist, with whom she has a second daughter, Lily, born in 1996. Kingsolver, her husband, and the two girls continue to live in Tucson. When she isn't writing, she spends her time parenting, cooking, gardening, and hiking. Because Kingsolver loves music, she sings and plays keyboard in several small groups, including an amateur rock band called the Rock Bottom Remainders, which is made up of fellow writers Stephen King, Amy Tan, and Dave Barry. Kingsolver continues to be an environmental activist and human rights advocate. She cherishes her role as a professional writer, which enables her to promote personal political and social agendas in hopes of leaving the world "a little more reasonable and just."

INTRODUCTION TO THE NOVEL

Two of the greatest influences in *The Bean Trees* are the Cherokee Trail of Tears, the geographical trek that the Cherokee Nation was forced to travel when it was moved to the Oklahoma territory from the southeastern United States, and the Sanctuary movement, designed to help Central Americans flee oppressive governmental regimes and relocate—usually secretly and illegally—in the United States. These two influences serve as the background to Kingsolver's *The Bean Trees*. The Cherokee Trail of Tears informs Taylor and Turtle's journey from Oklahoma to Arizona in the novel, and many of the novel's characters apparently are members of the Sanctuary movement.

The Cherokee Trail of Tears. By the end of the eighteenth century, the Cherokee Nation had settled on land guaranteed to it in a 1791 treaty with the United States. The land was located in northwest Georgia, eastern Tennessee, and southwest North Carolina. The Cherokees established a governmental system similar to that of the United States and adopted a constitution that declared them a sovereign nation, meaning that they were not subject to the laws of any other state or nation. They lived peacefully until gold was discovered on their land in the late 1820s.

Because the United States wanted the gold, in 1830, Congress passed the Indian Removal Act, which President Andrew Jackson immediately signed into law. The Cherokees fought removal by taking the case to the United States Supreme Court, which ruled in *Cherokee Nation v. Georgia* (1831) against the Cherokees because they were a "domestic dependent nation" and not a sovereign nation. On appeal, the case was heard once again in the Supreme Court, *Worcester v. Georgia* (1832), and the ruling was for the Cherokees, making the removal laws invalid. To be removed, the Cherokees would have to agree to removal and sign a treaty.

The Cherokee Nation was divided between moving and staying put. Most supported Chief John Ross, who fought against removal; however, about 500 Cherokees supported Major Ridge, who represented the United States government and advocated removal. In 1835, Ridge and members of the Cherokee treaty party signed the Treaty of New Echota. The treaty traded Cherokee land east of the Mississippi River for land in Indian Territory (the area that is now Oklahoma), plus more than five million dollars and other benefits from the federal government. The treaty, which was ratified by the United States Senate, gave the U.S. government and Georgia justification to force almost 17,000 Cherokees from their land.

In 1838, the U.S. Army began evicting the Cherokees from their homeland. Several thousand were taken immediately to Indian Territory. Thousands more were held in makeshift forts, having to make do with minimal food and facilities, until they were forced to march to Indian Territory during the winter of 1938-39. Approximately 4,000 Cherokees died during the march. The journey that the Cherokees took across land became known as the Trail of Tears, or the "trail where they cried."

The Sanctuary movement. Like the underground railroad that was established in the United States during the nineteenth century to assist runaway slaves, the Sanctuary movement was born in response to the plight of political refugees from the troubled Central American nations of El Salvador, Guatemala, Honduras, and Nicaragua.

The Sanctuary movement is an underground railroad that began in the United States in 1981 to help Central American citizens fleeing their homes to escape the repression, persecution, and violence of their governments. These Central American refugees traveled, often on foot, through Central America, into Mexico, and across the border into the United States. Because the Sanctuary movement can be successful only under complete secrecy, it is difficult to verify whether the movement remains vital today. Certain Central American governments still deny their citizens freedom to elect governmental officials, so odds are that the movement still operates.

The Central American political refugees received aid from religious communities located near the border. Aid took the form of food, shelter, and assistance with legal matters relating to the United States Department of Immigration and Naturalization Service (INS). The goal of these religious communities was to help the Central Americans obtain political asylum, enabling them to remain in the United States legally. The Central Americans could qualify for political asylum if they had proof of persecution. Because the Central Americans fled their homes, often with nothing but the clothing on their backs, they had no proof of persecution and were therefore denied political asylum. They were then deported—returned to their homeland to face persecution or, even worse, death.

The United States could not easily grant political asylum to Central Americans because it would mean openly admitting that Central Americans were being persecuted. It would also mean that the United States government would have to accept responsibility for some of the persecution. Under President Ronald Reagan, the U.S. government provided military and economic aid to military juntas (military groups that take control of a government at the conclusion of a revolution) in Central America, thereby sustaining the repression from which the political refugees were fleeing. As a result of friendly relations between the United States and Central

America, many Central American political refugees have been declared illegal aliens, and those who are not in sanctuary—hidden from governmental officials, who would force them to return to their native countries, and living secretly in the United States—have been deported.

It became clear to the religious communities that working within the legal system was not helping the political refugees. The refugees needed far more immediate assistance. In 1982, the Southside Presbyterian Church in Tucson, Arizona, and several churches in California declared themselves public sanctuaries for citizens of Guatemala and El Salvador. The Reverend John Fife, former minister of Southside Presbyterian Church, and Quaker Jim Corbett are credited with starting the underground-railroad form of refugee aid.

During the next two years, the Sanctuary movement grew. The Chicago Religious Task Force on Central America (CRTFCA) became the national coordinator for the underground railroad, and more than 300 churches and synagogues all over the United States became safe havens for political refugees. As many as 100,000 individuals became supporters of the Sanctuary movement despite the fact that they were breaking federal law by aiding illegal aliens and risking imprisonment and a fine of about $2,000. Starting out, the task force of the Sanctuary movement was overly cautious. Members changed cars frequently when transporting refugees from place to place, disguised the refugees, and followed complicated plans. The result resembled slapstick comedy and caused a great deal of confusion. Because the Immigration and Naturalization Service (INS) and Federal Bureau of Investigation (FBI) knew of the operation anyway, the task force decided to keep everything out in the open, but to be careful. For a while, the Sanctuary movement was protected by media attention, which brought to light the fact that refugees were being persecuted and that the U.S. government was sending these "illegal aliens" home to be murdered.

Finally, in 1984, several church workers were arrested in Texas and were charged with transporting illegal aliens. In 1985, sixteen sanctuary workers were arrested. Despite the efforts by the government to control the Sanctuary movement, the united community of sanctuary workers remains committed to providing aid to Central American political refugees.

A BRIEF SYNOPOSIS

Kingsolver wrote *The Bean Trees* in shifting points of view. All but two chapters of the novel are written in the first person, revealing the thoughts and feelings of the feisty protagonist, Taylor Greer. Kingsolver wrote Chapters 2 and 4 in limited third person (we see the character through the author's eyes rather than through the character's), presenting information as seen and understood by Lou Ann Ruiz, a significant character in the novel. The relationship that develops between Taylor and Lou Ann becomes a focus of the novel.

The Bean Trees begins when Taylor (whose real name is Marietta) decides that it's time to leave Pittman, Kentucky, where she lives with her mother, and make something of herself. She buys a 1955 Volkswagen and embarks on a personal journey of self-discovery, leaving everything behind, including her name. When her car runs out of gas in Taylorville, Illinois, she decides that her new name will be Taylor. From that point on, she is known as Taylor Greer.

In the middle of Oklahoma, on land owned by the Cherokee Nation, Taylor's car breaks down. Taylor stops to have it repaired and to get something to eat at a restaurant. Her life changes dramatically when, sitting in her car and ready to leave the restaurant and continue driving, a Cherokee woman puts a child wrapped in a blanket on the front seat of Taylor's car. The woman asks Taylor to take the child and then disappears in a pickup truck. Taylor suspects that the child, who doesn't speak, has been physically and sexually abused. Because the child holds onto Taylor's clothing with a fiercely determined grip that reminds Taylor of a mud turtle that won't let go of what it has in its mouth, Taylor names the child Turtle. Kingsolver introduces the perils of single motherhood as Taylor accepts her newfound responsibilities and makes a commitment—although Taylor is not fully aware that she has made such a commitment—to care for another human being.

Taylor and Turtle travel to Tucson, Arizona. Because of additional car problems, they end up at a business named Jesus Is Lord Used Tires. The owner of the business, Mattie, a courageous and kind person, eventually hires Taylor. Taylor soon discovers that

Mattie's shop is also a shelter for political refugees from Guatemala. After she befriends refugees Estevan and Esperanza, Taylor becomes more aware of discrimination and social injustice.

Looking for a place to live, Taylor responds to an ad in a newspaper and rents a room from Lou Ann Ruiz. An immediate bond forms between Taylor and Lou Ann when they realize that they both are from Kentucky. Lou Ann, whose husband just left her, and her young son, Dwayne Ray, and Taylor and Turtle provide a sense of family for each other. The women's friendship, the relationships that they develop with other characters, and the creation of a home in an unexpected place provide the main themes in the novel.

Eventually, the secure environment and the love that Taylor gives to Turtle pay off, and Turtle begins to speak. Her first word is "bean," and subsequent words are the names of vegetables. One day, when Turtle is in the park with Lou Ann and Taylor's neighbor, Edna, who is almost completely blind, someone grabs Turtle. Luckily, Edna has a cane and uses it to whack the perpetrator, setting Turtle free. Following the attack, Turtle withdraws and stops speaking. Because a social worker becomes involved in the case, it is discovered that Taylor has no legal right to Turtle and could lose her to the state if relatives are not found. Taylor, whose bond to Turtle is now no different than it would be if she were her natural mother, vows to take whatever steps are necessary to keep her daughter.

Taylor, along with Turtle, agrees to take Estevan and Esperanza to a safe house in Oklahoma. Once in Oklahoma, Taylor tries to find Turtle's relatives so that they can legally sign Turtle over to Taylor's care. Unfortunately, Turtle's relatives cannot be found. Unwilling to give up, Taylor asks Estevan and Esperanza for their help. They pose as Turtle's parents and express their wish to relinquish custody of their daughter to their friend, Taylor. Taylor adopts Turtle and then takes Estevan and Esperanza to the safe house. In the car on the way home to Tucson, Turtle names vegetables, this time including the names of the people in her family.

LIST OF CHARACTERS

Taylor Greer

The feisty protagonist of the novel. Taylor's real name is Marietta (Missy) Greer. A strong-willed and unpredictable young woman, she leaves her Kentucky home to begin a new life for herself. After her car breaks down in Oklahoma, she finds herself with a little girl to care for. She and the little girl, Turtle, end up in Tucson, Arizona. Taylor blossoms and matures as she becomes a caring mother and friend, learns about human rights and social injustice, and risks her life for people in need.

Alice Jean Stamper Greer

Taylor's mother, who supports herself and Taylor by working as a housekeeper for wealthy people. She maintains a positive attitude despite hard work and the responsibility of raising a child alone. Her love enables Taylor to become self-confident and independent.

Foster Greer

Taylor's father, who left home as soon as he found out that his wife was pregnant.

Eddie Rickett

Taylor's boss at her first "real" job in the lab at Pittman County Hospital.

Jolene Shanks

A girl Taylor knew from high school who got pregnant, dropped out of school, and married Newt Hardbine. Taylor talks to Jolene in the Pittman County Hospital while Jolene waits to have an x-ray taken after she is shot by her father-in-law.

Turtle

The three-year-old Cherokee child who is left on Taylor's car seat. After her mother's death, Turtle, whose real name is April, lived with her aunt and, during that time, apparently was physically and sexually abused by a male friend of her aunt. When she was left with Taylor, Turtle was catatonic: She blankly stared off into space, living in her own world and not speaking. Experiencing love from Taylor and others in the community, Turtle feels secure and safe enough to begin speaking. Her first words are the names of vegetables. Eventually, Turtle is adopted by Taylor.

Mrs. Hoge

The little old woman who works at the reception desk at the Broken Arrow Motor Lodge, where Taylor and Turtle stay temporarily on their way to Tucson. Mrs. Hoge helps her daughter-in-law, Irene, run the motel. She is kind to Taylor and Turtle, letting them stay in one of the rooms at the motor lodge during the Christmas holidays in return for Taylor's services as a chambermaid. She bickers with Irene and is disappointed because Irene hasn't given her a grandchild. Mrs. Hoge shakes a lot because she has Parkinson's disease.

Irene

Mrs. Hoge's daughter-in-law.

Mattie

A patient and kind widow who owns Jesus Is Lord Used Tires. An active participant in the Sanctuary movement, she uses her tire shop as a shelter for political refugees from Central America. She hires Taylor to work in her tire shop and becomes her friend.

Sandi

Sandi works at Burger Derby, where Taylor works briefly. She has a son named Seattle (after a racehorse named Seattle Slew). She loves horses and befriends Taylor when she learns that Taylor is from Kentucky. (Sandi thinks that everyone who lives in Kentucky has horses.)

Jessie

A homeless woman who takes leftover fruit and melon rinds from area coffee shops under the pretense that she needs them to paint still-lifes.

Timothy, Fei, and La-Isha

The people who put an ad in the newspaper for a roommate, which Taylor answers. They are vegetarians and participate in the New Age movement, drawing energy from cosmic sources.

Lou Ann Ruiz

Taylor's roommate and friend. She is separated from her husband and is raising their son alone. She is from Kentucky, and when Taylor answers her ad for a roommate, they become fast friends, and eventually family. Lou Ann is frightened of everything, is insecure, and has low self-esteem. With Taylor's encouragement and example, Lou Ann becomes more self-confident and self-directed.

Angel Ruiz

Lou Ann's estranged husband. As a result of an accident with his pickup truck, he lost a leg at the knee and has an artificial limb. After the accident, he becomes quite angry and blames others for things that they have no control over.

Dwayne Ray Ruiz

Lou Ann and Angel's son.

Ivy Logan

Lou Ann's mother, who lives in Kentucky with her mother-in-law, Granny Logan. She is prejudiced and didn't want Lou Ann to marry a Mexican.

Granny Logan

Lou Ann's grandmother, who lives in Kentucky with her daughter-in-law, Lou Ann's mother. She is demanding and prejudiced and rarely speaks directly to her daughter-in-law.

Bobby Bingo

An old man who sells fresh vegetables out of his run-down truck, which he parks down the street from where Lou Ann lives.

Lee Sing

The owner of the market across the street from where Lou Ann lives. She lives in the back of the store with her mother, who is said to be over a hundred years old.

Edna Poppy

A blind, elderly woman who lives with, and depends on, a woman named Virgie Mae. The two women are Taylor and Lou Ann's neighbors. Edna always dresses in red. She is a kind woman who occasionally baby-sits Turtle and Dwayne Ray.

Virgie Mae Valentine Parsons

Taylor and Lou Ann's neighbor. She is an extremely formal, rude, and prejudiced elderly woman who lives with and cares for Edna.

Father William

A priest involved with the Sanctuary movement.

Terry

A doctor who visits Jesus Is Lord Used Tires to care for the political refugees living in sanctuary. He eventually moves to a Navajo reservation to work.

Estevan

A political refugee from Guatemala living in sanctuary at Jesus Is Lord Used Tires. While in Guatemala, Estevan was an English teacher. He now washes dishes at a Chinese restaurant. Married to Esperanza, he risks his life to help Taylor keep Turtle by posing as Turtle's father.

Esperanza

Estevan's wife, who lives with him in sanctuary at Jesus Is Lord Used Tires. She is extremely depressed and attempts suicide. On the journey to the safe house in Oklahoma, Esperanza spends time caring for Turtle. She is able to symbolically give up her daughter, Ismene (who was kidnapped in Guatemala), when she poses as Turtle's mother and gives her to Taylor.

Harland Elleston

A man who marries Taylor's mother. He is part-owner of El-Jay's Paint and Body in Pittman County, Kentucky. According to Taylor, he has "warts on his elbows and those eyebrows that meet in the middle."

Cynthia

A social worker who becomes involved in Taylor and Turtle's lives when someone attempts to molest Turtle while she's under Taylor's care. Child Protective Services discovers that Taylor doesn't have legal claim to Turtle, and Cynthia informs Taylor. She later gives Taylor information about what she can do to acquire legal custody of Turtle.

Mr. Jonas Wilford Armistead

A tall, elderly man who arranges for Taylor's legal adoption of Turtle.

Mrs. Cleary

Mr. Armistead's secretary.

CRITICAL COMMENTARIES

CHAPTER 1

Kingsolver introduces the two major characters in the novel by writing Chapters 1 through 4 in alternating points of view. Chapters 1 and 3 (and the rest of the novel) are written in the first person. Taylor Greer, the spirited protagonist of the novel, tells the story from her perspective as she experiences and understands it. Chapters 2 and 4 are written in limited third person point of view—we see the character through the author's eyes rather than through the character's. In these two chapters, Kingsolver provides information as seen and understood by Lou Ann Ruiz, a major character in the novel.

In Chapter 1, we meet Taylor Greer (whose real name is Marietta). She was brought up, as was Kingsolver, in rural Kentucky among struggling tobacco farmers. She speaks a southern dialect that realistically imitates the dialect spoken by people who live in that part of rural Kentucky. Her dialect is full of colorful expressions—such as "I'll swan" and "ugly as a mud stick fence"—and imagery that compares unlikely things. For example, in the first paragraph of the novel, Taylor tells about her fear of putting air in tires. She describes a schoolmate's father who blew up a tractor tire by putting too much air in it. He got thrown over a Standard Oil sign and, according to Taylor, looked like "old overalls slung over a fence."

Taylor comes from a nontraditional family. She was raised by her mother, who worked long hours as a housekeeper to support Taylor and herself. Her father, Foster Greer, left her mother when he found out that her mother was pregnant. Her mother doesn't mind that Foster left; in fact, she often tells Taylor that "trading Foster for [you] was the best deal this side of the Jackson Purchase." As Taylor matures and is exposed to horrible things that fathers can say and do to children, she feels quite lucky to have grown up without a father. The resiliency of Taylor's mother and her commitment to Taylor, as well as her indifferent attitude toward men, represent Kingsolver's feminist views.

The importance of family, a major theme in the novel, is evident in the relationship between Taylor and her mother. Taylor's mother thinks that Taylor "hung up [the moon] in the sky and plugged in all the stars." She expects the best of Taylor, and Taylor doesn't disappoint her. Rather than get pregnant and drop out of high school like many of her classmates, Taylor finishes high school and is determined to make a life for herself. Her independent and courageous nature stems from the secure environment her mother provides. When Taylor feels as though she isn't good enough to ask for a job at the Pittman County Hospital lab, she talks to her mother, who boosts Taylor's morale and offers encouragement. Taylor asks for the job and ends up working in the lab for five and a half years. Later, when Taylor is working in the lab and has to help Jolene Shanks, an old schoolmate who's been shot by her father-in-law, and has to see Jolene's dead husband, the only place she wants to be is home so that she can tell her mother about the worst sight she has ever seen. Her mother creates a safe and supportive environment for Taylor, much like Taylor struggles to create for Turtle later in the novel.

Taylor's mother always tells Taylor that, as a last resort, they can "go live on the Cherokee Nation." Because Taylor's great-grandfather was a full-blooded Cherokee, they have "head rights" (a Native American tribe member's claim to tribal property). Here, Kingsolver refers to the Cherokee Trail of Tears when she mentions that Taylor's great-grandfather was "too old or too ornery to get marched over to Oklahoma," so he stayed in Tennessee.

The rural Kentucky setting in which *The Bean Trees* begins affords Kingsolver an opportunity to make use of her extensive background in biology and natural history. As a child, Taylor goes pond fishing. She catches blue gills and bass and watches the Jesus bugs walking on the surface of the water. Taylor and her mother have a colorful flower bed full of blooming marigolds and Hot Tamale cosmos. Another example of Kingsolver's biology background influencing the novel is Taylor's job in the Pittman County Hospital lab, which entails looking through a microscope to count red blood cells, testing urine, and helping with x-rays.

Taylor's resolve to leave Pittman County becomes a reality when she purchases a dilapidated 1955 Volkswagen. Ironically, the troubles she has with the car dramatically affect her life. Intending to travel beyond the borders of Kentucky, her car breaks down. Later, she gives herself a new name—Taylor—when her car almost runs out of gas in Taylorville, Illinois. When her car breaks down again, this time in Oklahoma, Taylor's feelings of despair and hopelessness as she views the flat terrain foreshadow the future.

After Taylor's car is repaired, she readies herself to leave Oklahoma forever. Ironically, she ends up with a Cherokee child on the seat beside her—ironic because "If [Taylor] wanted a baby [she] would have stayed in Kentucky." Not knowing what to do with the silent child wrapped in a blanket, Taylor drives down the highway. The novel's tone becomes serious as Taylor, experiencing an internal conflict between not wanting responsibility for a baby and not knowing where else to take it, questions her actions and realizes that she is totally responsible for the child. She feels some comfort in knowing that, if she needs help, she can always call 1-800-THE LORD, Oral Roberts' telephone number that flashed on the television screen in the restaurant where Taylor stopped.

Taylor is nervous about having the child with her in the car, particularly because the child appears to be catatonic—she doesn't speak, stares straight ahead, and rarely moves. Humorously, Taylor is relieved to see a sign of life when the child wets her pants. She passes a sign for the Pioneer Woman Museum, a metaphor for her life at the moment, and then stops at the Broken Arrow Motor Lodge. The name of the motor lodge is a metaphor for the child's "brokenness," which is a result of the abuse inflicted upon her during her short life.

Taylor resolves to care for the child and to protect her from future harm. She writes on a postcard to her mother, "I found my head rights, Mama. They're coming with me." This statement signals that Taylor has found something to connect her to her Indian heritage, which ultimately enables her to learn more about herself and mature emotionally.

(Here and in the following sections, difficult words and phrases are defined.)

- **pegged**   identified.
- **cut out of the same mud**   alike.
- **bringing home the bacon**   earning a salary.
- **moony**   romantically sentimental.

- **Candy Stripers** teenage volunteers in a hospital, noted for the requisite red-and-white striped uniforms that they wear.

- **Bobbie Brooks** a brand of clothing associated with well-to-do young adults.

- **Old Grand-Dad** a bourbon distilled in Kentucky.

- **Jackson Purchase** approximately 2,000 square miles of land that extended beyond the Tennessee River and became an addition to the state of Kentucky in 1818, when General Andrew Jackson and Isaac Shelby of the United States negotiated with the Chickasaw Indian Nation. The Chickasaws received $300,000 over fifteen years. (In the same treaty, the Chickasaws relinquished 6,000 square miles of land, which was added to the state of Tennessee.)

- **it was no horseradish** meaning no playing around.

- **Great Plain** high plateau in central North America; the High Plains in northwestern Oklahoma and the panhandle are part of the Great Plain.

- **cashing in and plowing under** committing suicide and being buried.

- **ace in the hole** something held in reserve that can help in an emergency.

- **head rights** claim to Native American ancestry.

- **Oral Roberts University** named for evangelist Oral Roberts and located in Tulsa, Oklahoma.

- **giant McDonald's thing** the stainless steel Gateway Arch in St. Louis, Missouri, which stands 630 feet tall and commemorates the city's role as the gateway to the West during the nineteenth century.

- **blue moon** the second full moon in a calendar month; "once in a blue moon" indicates a rare occurrence.

- **spit nails** angry.

- **plaits** braids.

- *Psycho* a 1960 Alfred Hitchcock movie about a murderous, mentally unbalanced man and one of his victims.

- **President Truman** Harry S. Truman (1884-1972), the thirty-third president of the United States (1945-1953).

CHAPTER 2

Kingsolver shifts the point of view in Chapter 2 to limited third person, relating information as it is seen and understood by Lou Ann Ruiz. Lou Ann, who, like Taylor, is a native Kentuckian, lives in Tucson, Arizona (an environment quite familiar to Kingsolver, who moved there in the late 1970s). Much to her mother's chagrin, Lou Ann married Angel Ruiz four years earlier. Soon after being married, they moved to Tucson to be close to Angel's family. Lou Ann's mother doesn't like Angel because he is Mexican: According to Lou Ann's mother, Mexicans are "trying to take over the world like the Catholics." Here, Kingsolver portrays the prejudice of Lou Ann's mother to reveal the fact that discrimination, in many forms, is prevalent in American society. Lou Ann tries to convince her mother that she is wrong about Mexicans by sending her newspaper clippings about successful Mexican people.

After being married for only a year, Angel has an accident in his truck. His leg is amputated at the knee, and he has to wear a prosthesis—an artificial leg—which "jingles" when he walks. Angel's amputated leg never bothers Lou Ann, but Angel can't accept it. He becomes dissatisfied with life and irritated by everything around him. When his relationship with Lou Ann falls apart, Lou Ann feels guilty because, in her mind, she's done nothing to try to save the marriage. She even thought about leaving herself, but it was easier to endure Angel's verbal abuse and just drift along. On Halloween, Angel cravenly packs his things and leaves Lou Ann while she is at her doctor's office for her seventh-month prenatal exam.

Many readers might object to the suggestion that Lou Ann feels guilty about Angel's walking out on her. Perhaps Lou Ann feels more indifferent about Angel's leaving her than she does guilty. Remember as you read the novel that the women in *The Bean Trees* ultimately survive—even flourish—without men in their lives. Kingsolver seems to suggest that women do not need men in their lives to feel self-worth.

Kingsolver uses Lou Ann's trip home from her doctor visit to bring to light feminist views regarding the sexual harassment of women and the struggle to survive that women face in a male-dominated society. The nurse in Lou Ann's doctor's office gives her a pamphlet about a diet that she is to follow. On the cover is a picture of a woman holding a baby. Lou Ann concludes that such pamphlets must be "put together by men" who don't like the looks of pregnant women; none of the many pamphlets she's received from her doctor's office have pictures of pregnant women. As Lou Ann rides the bus, men don't look at her directly, and males in general leave her alone. She decides that being able to ride a bus full of people without being sexually harassed is quite pleasant. Before she was pregnant, she couldn't ride the bus without being groped and taunted by men.

Walking home from the bus stop, Lou Ann passes Fanny Heaven, a pornography shop and club that advertises nude women and has a vulgar, "schoolchild"-like painting of a woman on the door. Every time she has to walk by Fanny Heaven, Lou Ann feels uncomfortable and tries to ignore it. Lou Ann's attempt to ignore Fanny Heaven emphasizes how she would rather pretend that something unpleasant doesn't exist than face it and try to change it. Unsure of herself, she discounts her own experiences and viewpoints, believing instead that she isn't strong enough to stand up for herself and to make a difference, not only in her own life, but also in others'. She's unwilling at this point in the novel to take risks.

Before going home, Lou Ann stops at Lee Sing's market to buy candy for trick-or-treaters (which she forgets to purchase), and food listed in the diet pamphlet for herself. She always feels a bit intimidated by Lee Sing because she makes "peculiar" comments. This feeling of intimidation recalls the feelings that Lou Ann has when she walks by Fanny Heaven. She will not—cannot—confront Lee Sing. This time, Lee Sing tells Lou Ann that she will probably have a girl because of the way she is carrying her baby. Lee Sing compares a baby girl to a "New Year pig" because it goes to someone else's family after being well fed. Lou Ann leaves the market feeling offended, but also guilty because she did just that—moved away from her own family after they raised her to be close to Angel's family in Arizona.

When Lou Ann gets home, she realizes that Angel has moved out. She wonders about the items he took and the things he left behind. The tone is sad as Lou Ann faces the reality of her situation. Unfortunately, she seems unable to do anything about her situation, teetering between accepting that she is now on her own and denying that Angel will not ultimately return.

- **Gumby doll**   a green rubber doll that can be bent in different directions.

- **conniption**   a fit of anger.

- **PCP**   phencyclidine; used by veterinarians as an anesthetic and used illegally as a psychedelic drug.

- **Angel Dust**   another name for PCP.

- **cyanide**   a poisonous compound.

CHAPTER 3

Kingsolver now shifts the point of view back to the first person and writes from Taylor's perspective. Taylor and the little girl, whom she names Turtle because the girl holds onto Taylor like a mud turtle, are on the road again, and Taylor is in "hog heaven." After staying at the Broken Arrow Motor Lodge through the Christmas holidays, Taylor decided to leave because her "eyes had started to hurt in Oklahoma from all that flat land." She's made some money working as a chambermaid while old Mrs. Hoge baby-sat Turtle.

To Taylor's discomfort, Mrs. Hoge insinuates that Turtle is retarded, but Taylor defends Turtle, as any committed, protective mother would, maintaining that Turtle has "her own ways of doing things." After Taylor and Turtle leave the Broken Arrow and Mrs. Hoge, the tone of the novel becomes more light and cheerful as Taylor and Turtle leave Oklahoma and eventually enter Arizona.

Kingsolver describes the Arizona desert landscape at sunrise by creating humorous images. "Puffy-looking rocks" are shaped like "roundish" people and animals, and "clouds are pink and fat and hilarious-looking, like the hippo ballerinas in a Disney movie." Because Taylor truly enjoys the physical environment of Arizona, she decides that she and Turtle will live there. Here, note how different environments affect Taylor throughout the novel. In rural Kentucky, she grew discouraged about living her entire life threatened by getting pregnant by men like Newt Hardbine (a newt is a type of salamander—certainly not a positive image of men). In

Oklahoma, Taylor grows weary of the never-ending landscape, symbolic of her wandering and meandering without something to tie her to the world. And in Arizona, with its natural beauty and peaceful colors, Taylor feels more at home.

As Taylor and Turtle drive through Tucson, Arizona, it begins to hail. The roads become icy and the car has no side windows, so Taylor pulls off the highway to seek cover and wait out the storm. Although she runs over glass on the off ramp and gets two flat tires, her spirits are not dampened. As she drives down the street, Taylor sees the Jesus Is Lord Used Tires shop.

Taylor stops her car and meets Mattie, a widow (another single woman) and owner of Jesus Is Lord Used Tires. Taylor finds out that both flat tires are irreparable; unfortunately, she can't even afford retreads. Noting her hesitancy, Mattie invites Taylor for a cup of coffee. Taylor accepts, and they go sit at a table in the back of the shop.

Kingsolver uses this scene in which Mattie initially greets Taylor and invites her to share in a cup of coffee to provide meaningful details that foreshadow the future. While Mattie gets Turtle some juice, a nervous-acting priest wearing blue jeans comes in looking for Mattie. He doesn't want to wait for Mattie and drives off in a car full of what look like "Indians." Mattie comes back with a spill-proof cup and, observing Taylor's inexperience with Turtle, casually mentions that Turtle could easily become dehydrated without enough to drink. When Taylor comments that Mattie must have grandchildren because she is so good with children, Mattie responds, "Something like that," without clarifying what she means. Here, Kingsolver presents Mattie as a somewhat mysterious person willing to help stranded travelers but unwilling to reveal much about herself. Only very late in the novel does Kingsolver better explain the reasons for Mattie's secrecy. However, note that Taylor doesn't seem all that alarmed by Mattie's unwillingness to explain herself. In fact, Taylor doesn't seem to notice the vagueness of Mattie's responses, perhaps because she already feels comfortable with this woman who unhesitatingly accepts her and Turtle.

Being around Mattie causes Taylor to look at her own lack of child-rearing skills. She feels incompetent as a parent and questions whether she is doing what is best for Turtle by keeping her.

Kingsolver interjects a feminist viewpoint as Mattie goes to assist a customer. Taylor watches her and feels proud to see that a woman is accepted for doing a "man's" job.

As Mattie and Taylor walk out to Mattie's garden, Taylor hears someone walking overhead without shoes on. This reference to someone overhead further emphasizes the mystery that surrounds Mattie. Again, however, Taylor trusts that Mattie is in control and knows what is upstairs. She is beginning to trust Mattie more and more.

Note that Kingsolver relies on her background in natural history to describe the bugs and spiders that surface after the hail and rain, as well as the vegetable and flower garden thriving in the dry, desert soil behind Mattie's tire shop. Kingsolver's biology background becomes evident when Taylor later inquires about work at the Red Cross plasma center and refuses to sell her blood because "Blood is the body's largest organ."

Taylor leaves her car at Mattie's and she and Turtle get a room at the Hotel Republic, within walking distance of Jesus Is Lord Used Tires. It is clear to Taylor that Tucson is nothing like rural Kentucky, where everyone knows everyone else and helps each other through good and bad times. Taylor feels lonely and depressed as she realizes that she and Turtle will have to "find [their] own way." Ironically, this struggle is necessary if Taylor is to mature as an adult and eventually recognize the human bonds between herself and the other women on whom she can rely. Earlier in the novel, when she still lived with her mother in Kentucky, Taylor relied totally on her mother for support and shied away from friendships with her schoolmates. Now, she cannot rely on her mother's protection and support and must learn to trust her own instincts.

The internal and external conflicts that Taylor experiences in Chapter 3 are representative of the struggle that many single mothers face. Taylor needs a job, but what can she do with Turtle when day care costs more than what she can earn? Where will she find a job with her limited experience? What if she can't provide for Turtle? What if her money runs out? How will they make it alone without family or friends to help? Also note that Kingsolver addresses the problem of teen pregnancy when Sandi, a young waitress at the Burger Derby restaurant, empathizes with Taylor, who describes Turtle as "just somebody I got stuck with."

- **Disney** meaning Walt Disney (1901-1966), the U.S. pioneer of animated film cartoons. The "hippo ballerinas" to which Kingsolver refers appear in the animated classic film *Fantasia* (1940).

- **doohickey** something whose name is unknown.

- **ORV** short for off-road vehicle; a camper known as a recreational vehicle (RV).

- **phlebotomist** a person trained to draw blood from people for diagnosis or study, or to determine how to treat a disease.

- **nineteen-ought-seven** 1907; *ought* is a colloquial word meaning *zero*.

- **the Derby** refers to the Kentucky Derby horse race, run annually near Louisville, Kentucky, on the first Saturday in May.

- **Secretariat** considered by many horse-racing fans the greatest racer ever; Secretariat won the coveted triple crown (the Kentucky Derby, the Preakness, and the Belmont Stakes) in 1973.

- **Seattle Slew** a race horse that won the Triple Crown in 1977.

- **towhead** a person with white or light-colored hair; tow is a coarse fiber used in the past to make gunnysacks.

CHAPTER 4

Once again, Kingsolver shifts points of view to limited third person. She also shifts the setting to Lou Ann's house in Tucson, Arizona. Lou Ann now has a baby boy named Dwayne Ray. Her mother (Ivy Logan) and grandmother (Granny Logan), both from Kentucky, are visiting to help Lou Ann with the new baby. Lou Ann asked Angel to move back into the house during the women's visit because she doesn't want to admit to her relatives that her marriage is over. Because Angel "[knows] the power of mothers and grandmothers," he does what she asks and they pretend to be a united family. Lou Ann doesn't like lying to her mother and grandmother, but she just can't reveal the truth about her failed marriage. Unfortunately, she is more worried about what *others* think and feel about her than she is about what she wants for herself. Rather than face conflict, she glosses over the problem by asking Angel to return home temporarily to further the appearance of a happy, picture-perfect marriage.

Throughout their two-week stay, Lou Ann's mother and grandmother do their best to avoid Angel. They help Lou Ann with the baby, and Granny Logan manages to complain about everything—from the Tucson heat to Lou Ann's moving far away from home and marrying a "heathern" Mexican who commits the sin of working on Sundays. She even insists on wearing her winter coat to the bus in eighty-degree heat simply because it's January—at home in Kentucky, it's cold. In describing Granny Logan, Kingsolver uses imagery similar to that found in poetry: "Her old hand pawed the air for a few seconds before Ivy silently caught it and corralled it in the heavy black sleeve."

Getting ready to leave for the bus, Lou Ann's mother brings her suitcase into the room. Lou Ann recognizes the leather belt holding it together: It is the same leather belt that her father used to whip her when she was young. Kingsolver includes this scene to continue to bring readers an awareness of child abuse.

The Kentucky dialect spoken by all three women is realistic. Lou Ann's mother and grandmother "have to git" for home, the bench at the bus stop is "hot as a poker," and without tea to drink on the bus, Granny Logan will be "dry as a old stick fence."

On her way home from the bus stop, Lou Ann stops to buy tomatoes from Bobby Bingo, who mentions that his son sells cars and is in television commercials. When he asks Lou Ann if she's ever seen one of the commercials, Lou Ann reveals that her husband left her and took the television with him, so she hasn't seen any of the commercials. Insightfully, she questions why she can tell the truth about her failed marriage to a stranger when she couldn't tell her own mother and grandmother. However, she doesn't ponder the answer long enough to gain a new awareness of herself.

Angel's coming home to pack his things and leave again prompts Lou Ann to recognize that she feels indifferent toward Angel. Whether or not Angel lives with her doesn't matter. Her feelings about Angel's presence contrast with the feelings she had when her mother and grandmother—women—were "filling up the house." Here, Lou Ann is beginning to recognize the strong female bonds between women, a theme that runs throughout the novel. Kingsolver seems to suggest that women do not abandon women; men do.

Angel's insensitivity toward Lou Ann is evident when he pours the Tug Fork water down the drain. Family members would have understood the sentimental value attached to the bottle of dirty water.

- **apoplectic** a stroke; a condition of great excitement or anger.

- **crosspatch** grouchy.

- **mustard plaster** a soothing treatment containing mustard.

- **grip** a suitcase.

- **heathe(r)n** an uncivilized or irreligious person.

- **crick** a creek.

- **tarnation** damnation.

CHAPTERS 5 & 6

Kingsolver shifts, for the last time, to a first person point of view, allowing Taylor to tell her own story as she experiences and perceives it. After eating breakfast at Burger Derby on several consecutive mornings and getting to know Sandi, a young waitress at the Derby, Taylor applies for and gets a job as a waitress there. She leaves Turtle at Kid Central Station, a baby-sitting service for shoppers at a local mall, while she's at work. The child care service is free, and Taylor and Sandi, whose son is there also, take turns going to check on their children. Although Taylor is fired from her job after only six days, at least she no longer has to leave Turtle at Kid Central, which she doesn't like. Perhaps unknowingly, Taylor is growing more protective of Turtle and more committed to motherhood.

Taylor begins scouring the local coffee shops for newspapers left lying on the tables for help-wanted and housing ads. A woman named Jessie, who claims leftover fruit and melon rinds, always has an "interesting-smelling shopping cart" with her and professes to be an artist, collecting the fruit "for still-lifes." Kingsolver uses Jessie to allude to homelessness.

Without a job, Taylor is unsure whether she can still afford the room at the Hotel Republic, so she begins looking not only for a job but a new place to stay. Kingsolver includes a comical sketch of individuals who are perceived as living on the fringe of society when she has Taylor meet three New-Agers looking for a roommate. Taylor can't imagine giving up toxins found in junk food or spending hours straining curd. She turns down a cup of alfalfa tea and humorously tells the three roommates that she and Turtle are going to "envision [themselves] in some other space."

At the next house, Taylor meets Lou Ann Ruiz. An immediate bond forms between them because they are both from Kentucky and speak the same dialect. Taylor and Lou Ann, both single mothers living at poverty level, decide to combine their resources and share Lou Ann's house. In effect, they create a community in which members are as concerned about others as they are about themselves. Aside from having children, the two mothers are quite different. Taylor is independent and spirited, whereas Lou Ann is fearful and feels worthless. Kingsolver again interjects humor to prevent the chapter's tone from becoming too depressing—Lou Ann and Taylor talk about Turtle, and Taylor notices Lou Ann's cat pawing at the carpet. Lou Ann thinks that the cat has a split personality because "the good cat wakes up and thinks the bad cat has just pooped on the rug."

Turtle's personality and demeanor haven't changed much in the time she's been with Taylor. Taylor understands that Turtle's experiences have had a major effect on her. When Taylor and Turtle first meet Lou Ann, Lou Ann whacks an ice tray against the counter to loosen the ice cubes and Turtle winces. Turtle's reaction suggests some previous emotional or physical abuse, but Kingsolver refrains from explaining the girl's obviously painful past.

When Lou Ann talks about her fear of flying and a particular airplane crash, Taylor recalls that she earlier saw on the news that the only survivor of the crash, a flight attendant, was rescued by a rope that had been dropped to her from a helicopter. The look on Turtle's face reminds Taylor of the look on the flight attendant's face as she gripped the rope. Although Taylor is growing more and more protective of Turtle, she cannot yet understand the causes for Turtle's mysterious actions. Later, when Lou Ann asks Taylor if Turtle is adopted, Kingsolver foreshadows the future because people don't "just dump [a baby] like an extra puppy."

Taylor's Route t

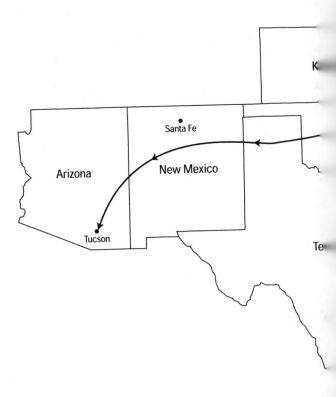

① Marietta Greer leaves fictitious Pittman County, Kentuck

② Marietta's car runs out of gas in Taylorville; to reward
herself for leaving Kentucky, she renames herself "Taylor

③ According to Taylor, she turns south at Wichita, Kansas.

Taylor's car breaks down on the Cherokee Nation, in Oklahoma, where a mysterious woman gives Taylor a baby. Taylor and the baby, whom she names Turtle, temporarily stay at the Broken Arrow Motor Lodge.

Taylor and Turtle reach Tucson, where they begin a new life, surrounded by many supportive friends. Taylor briefly drives to Oklahoma City to adopt Turtle formally, but she is on her way back to Tucson when the novel ends.

Despite her fear of exploding tires, Taylor starts working for Mattie at Jesus Is Lord Used Tires. Taylor seems able to face her fears and work to overcome them, especially if it means being able to support Turtle monetarily and emotionally. Mattie agrees to give Taylor two tires for her Volkswagen and help fix the ignition, so she can't refuse the job offer. Noticing that Taylor is jumpy around loud noises, Mattie asks her if she's "running from the law." Foreshadowing the future, Mattie comments, "I've got enough of that on my hands," without explaining any further. Embarrassed, Taylor admits to being afraid of exploding tires. Kingsolver's scientific background is again evident as Mattie helps Taylor overcome her fear of exploding tires by performing an experiment and explaining exploding tires in relative terms.

As time passes, Taylor becomes more aware of Spanish-speaking people living with Mattie. The people come and go with the blue-jeaned priest whom Taylor met on her first visit to Mattie's shop. When Taylor asks Mattie about the people, Mattie asks her if she knows what a sanctuary is. Taylor's only familiarity is with sanctuaries set aside to protect birds. Mattie tells her that sanctuaries exist for people, too. Here, Kingsolver begins focusing Taylor's—and the reader's—attention on the plight of less fortunate people. Taylor's growing awareness of the world around her mirrors her newfound awareness of herself as a responsible adult in whose care a young girl has been placed.

Taylor comes home from her job at Mattie's one evening and is upset because it is as if she and Turtle and Lou Ann and Dwayne Ray have become a *family*. She goes to work while Lou Ann stays home and cooks, cleans, and takes care of the children. Taylor's reaction reveals her independence but also shows that she still has some maturing to do; through Turtle, she is still learning how to open up to and care for other people. Taylor voices her feelings, and naturally, Lou Ann feels bad and cries. She wants to please Taylor because she doesn't want Taylor to abandon her like Angel did. Kingsolver's feminist views and humor become more apparent as Taylor tells Lou Ann her theory about not staying with one man for an entire lifetime. Taylor compares men to the flapper ball that shuts off the water in a toilet tank. Taylor had memorized a line from a flapper ball package that read, "Parts are included for all installations, but no installation requires all of the parts." Taylor doesn't think "there's an installation out there that could use all of [her] parts." She also shows Lou Ann a Valentine card that she bought for her mother. On the outside, the card reads, "Here's hoping you'll soon have something big and strong around the house to open those tight jar lids." On the inside is a picture of a pipe wrench. Taylor doesn't dislike men; her attitude is one of indifference—a major theme in the novel. Taylor and Lou Ann laugh, and Lou Ann is in disbelief as she realizes that Taylor has stayed up half the night to talk out a problem with *her*.

Throughout Chapters 5 and 6, Kingsolver continues to use her extensive background in biology and natural history to create images and symbols. For example, she compares the railroad system in Tucson to a hardened artery in a human body. At one time, the railroad probably brought new life to the city "like a blood vessel carrying platelets to circulate through the lungs." After a frost kills Mattie's purple beans, Mattie tells Taylor, "That's the cycle of life . . . the old has to pass on before the new can come around."

The tone at the conclusion of Chapter 6 is happy. Taylor and Lou Ann survive their first "talk" and realize that they have become friends.

- **freeloader**   a person who imposes on another's hospitality without sharing in the responsibility or cost.

- **Mr. Ed**   a popular television show in the early 1960s whose title character was a talking horse. (The "horse" was actually a trained zebra.)

- **hunkered**   crouched down.

- **Beach Blanket Bingo**   refers to a 1965 beach movie of the same name, featuring teen idols Frankie Avalon and Annette Funicello.

- **homeostasis**   a relatively stable state of equilibrium.

- **sarong**   a long strip of cloth worn as a dress or skirt.

- **flex**   short for *flexible*.

- **splitting our gussets**   laughing hard enough to rip the seams in your clothing.

- **Junebug**   a large beetle.

- **jerry can**   a container that holds about five gallons of liquid.

- **foisting**   deceitfully forcing someone to accept something.

- **Blondie and Dagwood**   a married couple in a newspaper comic strip.

- **Heimlich Maneuver**   an abdominal thrust to dislodge food or other material from a choking person's windpipe.

- **José Cuervo**   a brand of tequila.

- **star sapphire**   a gem cut and polished to show a star shape in the stone.

- **Sing Sing**   a U.S. federal penitentiary located in Ossining, New York.

CHAPTERS 7 & 8

Taylor's commitment to Turtle becomes a priority in her life. Returning home from a picnic in the desert, Taylor has to stop the car quickly because a mother quail and her babies are crossing the road. Kingsolver includes this episode to emphasize the responsibilities of motherhood and how Taylor is beginning to accept them. Taylor feels as proud as any parent when Turtle laughs and smiles for the first time after turning a somersault when the car stops quickly. And later, when Taylor and Turtle are in Mattie's garden planting seeds, Turtle says her first word, "bean." Taylor hugs Turtle and tells her—as her own mother told her—that she is "just about the smartest kid alive." Here, Taylor supports Turtle as her mother supported her while she was growing up in Kentucky. Her "smartest kid alive" comment suggests that she will succeed in raising Turtle to be a self-sufficient woman, just like her mother raised her.

Turtle, whose real name Taylor and Lou Ann discover is April, is as "healthy as corn," a metaphor that likens Turtle to a vegetable, which is the only class of words that Turtle seems able—or willing—to say. However, taking her role as a mother seriously, Taylor thinks that because of the abuse Turtle endured, Turtle should be examined by a doctor. Taylor takes her to Lou Ann's doctor and learns that Turtle is close to three years old, not two as she'd guessed. The doctor points out the many bones that have been broken and healed in Turtle's little body. Because this information is more than Taylor can bear, she stares out the window that the x-rays are propped up against. Seeing a bird's nest in a thorny cactus, she wonders how the bird ever "made a home in there." The bird's nest in the cactus symbolizes the miracle of Turtle's survival. Somehow, Turtle made a "home" within herself and survived.

Although the doctor tells Taylor that Turtle has a condition called "failure to thrive," wherein a physically or emotionally deprived child stops growing, he admits that the condition is reversible. Taylor knows that Turtle is growing physically because she buys her new, larger-sized clothes, but Taylor does not take sole responsibility for Turtle's emotional and psychological progress and well-being. Here, the themes of family and community are evident: Without the help of her "family," including Lou Ann, Taylor would not be the mother she's learned to become.

Taylor's extended family also includes her elderly neighbors, Edna Poppy and Virgie Mae Parsons. She and Lou Ann leave the children with Edna and Virgie Mae whenever they have an emergency or whenever neither one can be at home to care for the children. Gradually, Taylor and Lou Ann grow to depend on Edna and Virgie Mae to baby-sit. By introducing the two older women, Kingsolver again emphasizes the community of women needed to raise children. Note the irony in the differences between the two elderly women: Edna is a kind woman who always dresses in red from head to foot. Her sweet nature makes up for Virgie Mae, who is a prejudiced, narrow-minded person. However, together the women survive by serving as balancing forces for each other.

Taylor also meets Esperanza and Estevan, a young married couple from Guatemala City, who are living with Mattie. Estevan taught English in Guatemala and is now washing dishes in a Chinese restaurant in Tucson (something Taylor doesn't quite understand), and Esperanza spends her time upstairs at Mattie's. Esperanza reminds Taylor of Turtle: She sits very still, as though she's in her own world. Kingsolver hints that Esperanza might have survived traumatic times also. When Esperanza first meets Turtle, she looks and acts shocked and can't stop looking at her. Later, Estevan explains that Turtle reminds Esperanza of a child they knew in Guatemala.

Working at Jesus Is Lord Used Tires, Taylor can't help but observe the people living at Mattie's. She begins to understand that Jesus Is Lord Used Tires is more than a tire shop; it is also a hiding place for refugees. People come and go quietly. A doctor named

Terry comes on a bicycle and treats the people who are sick or hurt. Mattie explains that, many times, the people have been burned with cigarettes. Taylor soon realizes that these people have been tortured. Many times, Mattie goes away for weeks at a time, claiming that she's "birdwatching." Taylor understands that Mattie's missions are related to the people living in the rooms above the tire shop. However, Kingsolver does not yet explain the details surrounding the reasons refugees like Estevan and Esperanza seek political freedom in the United States.

One evening, Taylor and Lou Ann learn that Mattie is going to be on the evening news, and they invite Esperanza and Estevan, who have become their friends, and Edna and Virgie Mae to watch Mattie on the news and have dinner. Because Angel took Lou Ann's television when he left, Edna and Virgie Mae bring their television. Surprised, they listen as Mattie discusses human rights, the legal obligation of the United States to help people whose lives are in danger, and the fact that most Guatemalans and Salvadorans are not granted asylum—that is, they are not allowed to stay in the United States legally.

Unfortunately, the situation at Taylor and Lou Ann's is rather chaotic, and Lou Ann completely misses the broadcast. When she asks what Mattie said on television, Virgie Mae replies that it was just about "some kind of trouble with illegal aliens and dope peddlers." Aware of how culturally prejudiced Virgie Mae is, Estevan introduces himself and Esperanza to Edna and Virgie Mae as "Steven" and "Hope." They do not reveal their real names, and Taylor begins to understand the seriousness of the Sanctuary movement. Note that when Estevan comments that he and "Hope" have no children, Esperanza reacts as though she has been slapped. Here, Esperanza's reaction and her behavior toward and around Turtle are mysterious—as mysterious as her and Estevan's identities.

Virgie Mae makes it quite clear that as far as she is concerned, foreigners should stay in their own countries because they are not welcome in the United States. Taylor is appalled at Virgie Mae's rudeness, but ironically, Estevan doesn't appear to be bothered. Instead of being offended, he tells a story about people helping each other, which is symbolic of the interdependence among people from all walks of life.

Taylor's relationships with her newfound extended family and community continue to strengthen as she shares experiences with them. For example, when she apologizes to Estevan for Virgie Mae's unkind words, Estevan comments that he understands—because he has obviously encountered before—the older woman's racism: "Americans . . . believe that if something terrible happens to someone, they must have deserved it." Insightfully, Taylor responds, "I guess it makes us feel safe." Here, Kingsolver uses Taylor and Estevan's conversation to bring awareness to readers about social issues such as human rights and discrimination. She reinforces the fact that bad things do happen in life; however, people have to be prepared to help each other, not stand on the sidelines and hope that other people's misfortunes won't affect them.

Taylor and Lou Ann talk freely to each other. Sitting in Roosevelt Park (also known humorously as Dog Doo Park) under the arbor of wisteria vines, they discuss the upcoming marriage of Taylor's mother. Taylor can't imagine her mother getting married. Once again, Kingsolver portrays certain feminist views regarding men as Lou Ann comments that Taylor characterizes men as "hangnail[s]." Taylor denies Lou Ann's accusations and admits to liking Estevan. Lou Ann talks about Angel and admits that she'd go back to him if he asked her. Ironically, Angel does show up, but rather than ask for a reconciliation, he asks for a divorce. As Taylor and Lou Ann sit in the park, a child peddles by on a tricycle. Here, Kingsolver suggests future events as the child tells the two women to beware of "the bums" and "go straight home."

In these two chapters, Kingsolver once again uses her background in natural history to create poetic images. For example, the miracle of Dog Doo Park is "a purplish lip of petal stuck out like a pout from a fat green bud"—the beautiful flowers that sprout from the wisteria vines out of bare dirt. At the hideaway in the desert, white rocks protrude from the water's surface like "giant, friendly hippo butts," and cottonwood trees "cooled their heels" in the water.

- **rutabagas** root vegetables, similar to turnips, with white- or yellow-colored flesh.

- **Sherman tank** a large, armored military vehicle that runs on treads instead of wheels.

- **Jesus bugs**   insects that skim across the top of water.

- **discombobble**   confuse or upset.

- **picayune**   unimportant.

- **hypochondriac**   needlessly worrying.

- **Tortolita**   Spanish, meaning *little turtledove.*

- **mange**   a skin disease, common to mammals, characterized by lesions, itching, and hair loss.

- **succotash**   a corn and lima bean dish.

- **Burpee's catalogue**   Burpee is a company that sells plants and seeds to gardeners through a catalogue.

- **constitutional**   a walk taken for health reasons.

- **midi-skirt**   a skirt that reaches mid-calf.

- **Eleanor**   refers to Eleanor Roosevelt (1884-1962), activist, humanitarian, and wife of U.S. President Franklin D. Roosevelt.

- **scabies**   a contagious rash caused by mites.

- **spiral fibular fracture**   a type of break in the fibula, a bone running from the knee to the ankle.

CHAPTERS 9 & 10

In Chapters 9 and 10, Taylor is confronted with issues concerning people who suffer through no fault of their own. At the beginning of Chapter 9, Estevan shows up on Taylor's doorstep to tell her that Esperanza has tried to commit suicide. Taylor notes that Estevan is deeply troubled, that "something inside this man [is] turning inside out." Nervous and not knowing how to respond, she warns Estevan that she will either "shove food at [him] or run on at the mouth." Trying to console Estevan (and herself), she tells Estevan about a boy she knew in high school who killed himself with electrical wires. He had been a misfit, not belonging to any of the "in" groups in school. Taylor also discusses a group of school kids condescendingly referred to as Nutters, a group of poor kids who picked walnuts to earn money, were not a popular group, but "had each other." By having Taylor discuss the many contentious social groups commonly found in high schools, Kingsolver emphasizes the interdependency between people and how necessary it is to be a member of a community.

Kingsolver presents much of the political background surrounding Estevan and Esperanza. Estevan tells a shocked Taylor about how he was tortured in Guatemala with the electrical wires in field telephones made in the United States. He also explains that Turtle looks like Ismene, Estevan and Esperanza's daughter, who was kidnapped during a raid on their village. Taylor finds it incredible that Estevan and Esperanza chose to save the lives of seventeen other people and leave Guatemala rather than risk their lives or the lives of others to find Ismene.

Faced with the atrocities that Estevan describes, Taylor cannot even imagine having to make such a horrific decision as Estevan and Esperanza have had to make. To think that she lives in the same world in which these atrocities take place is almost too much for her to bear. She had never paid attention to what was going on outside her own life. She now realizes that the things she'd tried her hardest to avoid—exploding tires and motherhood—have become blessings because she's met Mattie and has Turtle.

Although Taylor is attracted to Estevan, she respects his marriage to Esperanza and treats him as a friend. During the night, as she sits on the couch with Estevan, Turtle, and the cat, Taylor is reminded of the paper dolls she'd played with as a child—the Family of Dolls. The Family of Dolls was the "perfect" family. It crosses Taylor's mind that they could have been the Family of Dolls in a different life. The tone is sad because she realizes that a Family of Dolls is not within her reach: She knows too much about the world around her. Here, in these chapters, Taylor discovers a new awareness within herself. There is no such thing as a "perfect" family; the families that she's been part of—first with her mother and now with an extended, nontraditional family—might not be picture-perfect, but they provide the emotional support that she needs to live a successful life.

When Taylor goes to see Esperanza in the room above Mattie's, she is unsure of how to console Esperanza. She talks about Turtle and Turtle's capacity for understanding even though she appears to be in her own little world. Importantly, she also tells Esperanza that she knows about Ismene. Taylor's character has become more complex as she has gained awareness of the atrocities that occur in the world around her. Discussing how hard it is to lose a loved one, she intuitively says to Esperanza, "Some people never have anybody to lose, and . . . that's got to be so much worse."

Taylor's new perceptions of the world also include the people immediately around her. For example, she discovers that Edna Poppy is blind and has been for years, which is why Edna always dresses in red—Edna never has to worry about her clothes matching—and why it appears that Edna always looks over the top of the head of the person she talks to. Edna has learned that, to survive, she must depend on other people. She depends on Virgie Mae daily, and she depends on Taylor to tell her what she is buying in Lee Sing's market. By recognizing that she cannot survive alone, she has rendered her disability unnoticeable.

The important and necessary interdependency among people is evident in the relationship between Taylor and Lou Ann. Taylor's independent, tough-acting personality tends to rub off on Lou Ann, who is generally timid and meek. For the first time, Lou Ann steadfastly maintains her own opinion when she and Taylor discuss what they think a bird is saying. And when Taylor is upset because Lou Ann had to endure sexual harassment in a recent job interview, Lou Ann comments that Taylor never lets anyone take advantage of her. Taylor is a positive influence on Lou Ann. She won't allow Lou Ann to be put down by anyone, nor will she allow Lou Ann to put *herself* down.

Despite the suffering that people endure, miracles do happen. For example, while Taylor, Turtle, Lou Ann, and Dwayne Ray are sitting under the arbor in Roosevelt Park, Turtle looks up at the wisteria flowers and says, "Beans." Taylor and Lou Ann try to explain that the buzz is from a bee. Turtle points and says, "Bean trees." She is right. The wisteria flowers that have gone to seed look just like beans.

- **caste system** divisions within a society based on differences in wealth, occupation, or inherited position.

- **disintegrated** broken apart.

- **conjecture** a conclusion arrived at by guesswork.

- **ipecac**   a shrub whose roots are used as a medicine that induces vomiting.

- **"La Bamba"**   a Mexican song made popular in the U.S. by Ritchie Valens.

- **beef shingles on toast**   a dish in which dried beef is cooked in a gravy and then poured over toast.

- **before you can say Jack Robinson**   an expression to reflect that an event happened quickly.

- **wainscoting**   wooden paneling.

- **croup**   a type of laryngitis marked by difficulty in breathing and a hoarse cough.

- **higgledy-piggledy**   confused; in disarray.

- **flotsam and jetsam**   a phrase used to describe objects either floating or washed ashore; an image of chaotic mess.

- **hex**   a jinx or an evil spell.

CHAPTERS 11 & 12

Lou Ann's self-confidence increases when she begins working at Red Hot Mama's salsa factory. Within no time she receives a promotion. Because of Lou Ann's more positive self-image, Taylor enjoys her company more than usual. However, Lou Ann still feels that she is "completely screwed up." She always looks for disasters and worries about things that haven't happened. For example, she relates a dream about Dwayne Ray to Taylor in which an angel came to her and said that her baby wouldn't live very long. This dream is one reason she is so protective of Dwayne Ray.

In these chapters, the tone changes from contentment to bewilderment, for everything seems to be changing at once. Lou Ann receives gifts from Angel and an invitation to live with him in Montana. Terry, the doctor who takes care of the people in Mattie's sanctuary, has moved to a Navajo reservation. The priest, Father William, who transports the people to and from Mattie's, is overly nervous. And Mattie goes "birdwatching" often and is hardly ever home; when she is home, she talks about "trouble in the air." We also learn that Estevan and Esperanza have to move to another safe house or they will be arrested, deported, and probably killed.

Although Taylor instinctively wants to minimize the injustices in the world that Estevan and Esperanza's plight symbolizes, she must at least acknowledge their existence, for people in her community whom she has come to love are being affected.

Taylor's experiences cause her to mature. Chapter 12 begins with a joyful tone as Mattie takes Taylor, Estevan, and Esperanza to the desert to witness the coming of rain. In this scene, Kingsolver again uses her natural history and biology background to create a spectacular sight in which she likens the desert plain to a "palm stretched out for a fortuneteller to read." She describes lightning as "white ribbons" and personifies the mesquite trees as able to "shiver," much like a person who is cold would. The rain falls, and after months of sun, it is an unbelievable relief. After dancing in the rain, the group makes its way back to Mattie's truck and heads home.

The peaceful and idyllic feeling is abruptly shattered and changed to frustration, anger, and despair when Taylor finds out that Turtle was hurt while in the park with Edna. Ironically, Taylor can't console the traumatized Turtle because she herself is overwhelmed with guilt. Instead, she helps Virgie Mae free a bird trapped in the house, a symbolic representation of Taylor's wish to free Turtle from her catatonic state. Luckily, Turtle wasn't molested. She has a bruise and was a bit shaken up. Although a social worker tells Taylor that Turtle will most likely speak again, as children are quite resilient, the social worker's encouragement does nothing to relieve Taylor's feelings of despair. She feels that she is an incompetent mother because she wasn't able to protect Turtle. Overwhelmed with the "ugliness" in the world, she is upset about people hurting children, people hurting people who can't fight back, and people not feeling sorry for other people anymore. Her world has changed, and she has difficulty knowing what to do about it.

- **cilantro** a leafy herb popular in Mexican and Italian cooking.

- **cicadas** a type of insect; male cicadas make a loud buzzing sound by rubbing body parts together.

- **Keno** a bingo-type lottery game.

- **Quickdraw McGraw** a cartoon horse that was a sheriff in the south-western desert of the U.S.

- **pungent** having a sharp odor.

- **catatonic** lacking activity, movement, or expression.

- **anatomical** resembling the human body.

CHAPTER 13

In this chapter, things go from bad to worse. Taylor finds out from Cynthia, the social worker, that because she doesn't have a legal claim to Turtle, the state of Arizona could take Turtle away from her. Because she already blames herself for what happened to Turtle in the park and feels inadequate as a parent, Taylor contemplates withdrawing into a protective shell and denying that she has responsibilities to people other than herself. She feels victimized. However, Kingsolver reverses the roles that she's established for her main characters by having Lou Ann, who is usually the victim, get mad at Taylor. Here, Kingsolver once again emphasizes the important interdependence between people. Lou Ann tells Taylor to do what Taylor has told her to do: to stand up and fight. Lou Ann's uncharacteristic reaction underscores the fact that Taylor, Lou Ann, and their children have become a family. They stick up for each other and prove that family values prevail over unjust laws.

Taylor is relieved when, after only a few weeks, Turtle begins to speak again. During visits to the social worker, Turtle plays with the anatomically correct dolls and often puts them under the blotter on Cynthia's desk. Note that Taylor is convinced that Turtle is "planting" the dolls. Here, Kingsolver foreshadows the future as Cynthia expresses her concern about Turtle "burying" the dolls.

Confused about what would be best for Turtle, Taylor talks to Mattie, who encourages Taylor to look at the situation from a different perspective: to ask herself whether she wants to try to raise Turtle. Taylor and Mattie's conversation emphasizes that mothers can only do their best to keep their children safe; nobody can protect a child from the world.

During a visit from Taylor, Cynthia realizes that Taylor has made the decision to keep Turtle and gives Taylor the name of a man to contact in Oklahoma after she locates Turtle's relatives.

Note that Taylor asks Cynthia about the cameo brooch that Cynthia often wears, wondering if Cynthia has to shop at the Salvation Army because she doesn't have a lot of money or if she likes "rummaging through other people's family heirlooms." Taylor's comment is a metaphor for Cynthia's job as a social worker.

Taylor decides that she and Turtle will go to Oklahoma to find Turtle's relatives so that Taylor can adopt her. Taylor will also take Estevan and Esperanza to a safe house in Oklahoma. Kingsolver creates suspense as Mattie discusses the penalties involved in transporting illegal immigrants, including jail and stiff fines. Esperanza and Estevan will be deported and killed. And Turtle will be taken away from Taylor. However, to her credit, Taylor is not swayed from her decision.

Kingsolver balances the ugliness of the world that Taylor has to endure with the beauty of nature. The night before Taylor, Turtle, Estevan, and Esperanza are to leave for Oklahoma, Virgie Mae comes to Taylor and Lou Ann's door saying that she wants to show them something. Taylor and Lou Ann wake the children and take them to Edna and Virgie's front porch, where they see the most beautiful night-blooming cereus, a plant that blooms only one night each year. The sight portends a positive outcome to Taylor's trip to Oklahoma, according to Lou Ann. "Something good" will happen.

Note that Mattie gives Taylor an envelope full of money before Taylor sets out for Oklahoma. Here, Mattie acknowledges that different people play different roles in life: Some people take risks, succeed, and are called heroes; others work behind the scene but are as important as the more public heroes. To Mattie, what Taylor is doing is heroic.

- **coerced**   forced.

- **notarized**   certified as authentic by a public officer.

CHAPTERS 14 & 15

The level of suspense and tension increases as Taylor, Turtle, Estevan, and Esperanza leave Tucson in a car. Esperanza rides in the backseat with Turtle. Esperanza's long hair is flowing free of the braid she usually wears, ironically portraying a "brave show of freedom." At the New Mexico border, they are stopped by Immigration officers for a routine car check. Because Taylor is guilty of transporting illegal immigrants and Estevan and Esperanza *are* illegal immigrants, they are all extremely nervous. However, their interaction with the patrol officer turns out to be routine and uneventful. Note that when the officer asks who the parents of Turtle are, Estevan claims her as his and Esperanza's.

Throughout the trip, Taylor feels increasingly uncomfortable about the relationship developing between Esperanza and Turtle. She has to do all the driving, so she is grateful that Esperanza plays with Turtle, but as she watches them in the rearview mirror, she thinks that she hears Esperanza call Turtle "Ismene." Kingsolver creates a sense of foreboding as Taylor begins to get upset about the affection that Esperanza and Turtle apparently have for each other.

The dialogue between Taylor and Estevan in the car emphasizes the issue of social injustice and the themes of family and community. Much of their discussion is about national symbols. Estevan asks if the alligator on his shirt (the Izod logo) is a symbol of the United States, and Taylor insightfully thinks that it could be an appropriate symbol because the United States is as capable of hurting people as an alligator is. Estevan tells Taylor that the national symbol of Guatemala is a bird called the quetzal. The quetzal dies if it is kept in a cage, similar to the Central American people who are dying because they do not have personal freedoms. Estevan also talks about the atrocities that the police are guilty of in Guatemala—how they burn villages and crops in order to wear down the people. The people become so tired from moving and starting over that they can no longer fight for freedom. Discussing what "home" means, Estevan feels unwanted everywhere. Here, Kingsolver makes it clear that home is wherever you settle and develop interdependent relationships that form a community.

When they reach Oklahoma, Estevan and Esperanza decide to spend an additional day with Taylor and Turtle while Taylor looks for Turtle's relatives. Taylor is experiencing internal and external conflicts. She is scared. A part of her doesn't want to find Turtle's relatives because they might want Turtle, but if she doesn't find them, she'll lose Turtle anyway. She has no choice. Because Taylor doesn't know what to expect and doesn't know what to think of the situation she finds herself in, she thinks about what is safe, secure, and predictable. She misses her old, beat-up car and Lou Ann. She misses home. When she finally locates the restaurant where she first received Turtle from Turtle's mysterious aunt, she courageously goes inside and soon realizes that finding any of Turtle's relatives will be impossible. She wishes that Lou Ann were with her, telling her not to give up hope. Ironically, she's now emotionally dependent on Lou Ann much like Lou Ann is on her. More and more, Taylor is realizing her need for and dependence on a sense of "home," which Lou Ann represents.

At the lush-green Lake o' the Cherokees, where the group takes a one-day vacation, Taylor realizes that she has adapted to the Arizona desert but still misses the green foliage and the mountains of her native Kentucky. However, note that she doesn't contemplate moving back to Kentucky; Tucson is now her home.

At the lake, something changes in Esperanza. Incorporating a metaphor about spring in Alaska—the rivers beginning to run and huge chunks of ice breaking apart and shifting—Kingsolver describes Esperanza: Her eyes look clear, and when she speaks, she looks directly into Estevan's and Taylor's eyes.

During their picnic at the lake, Taylor sees Turtle burying her doll. She explains to Turtle that dolls don't grow when they are planted. When Turtle says "Mama," Taylor finally realizes that Turtle must have seen her mother buried. (Recall that earlier in Chapter 15, as Taylor drove past a cemetery, Turtle pointed at the cemetery out of the car window and said, "Mama," although at the time Taylor didn't understand the significance of Turtle's action.) Finally realizing the deep emotions that Turtle no doubt experienced when her mother died, Taylor determines to "try as hard as I can" to keep Turtle. She makes a commitment to Turtle and acknowledges that she will fight for her no matter what.

Kingsolver heightens the novel's suspense as Estevan and Esperanza agree to risk their lives for Taylor and Turtle.

- **culottes**   loose-fitting women's shorts cut below the knee, resembling skirts.

- **Border Patrol**   a U.S. federal agency that works to keep illegal immigrants out of the country.

- **Aesop's Fables**   a collection of morality tales often read to children.

- **Parkinson's disease**   a progressive disease, marked by shaking, that affects the nervous system.

CHAPTERS 16 & 17

Chapter 16 is the climactic chapter in the novel. Estevan, Esperanza, Taylor, and Turtle visit Mr. Armistead, the person whom Cynthia, the social worker, suggested that Taylor see about getting legal guardianship of Turtle. In Armistead's office, Estevan and Esperanza pretend to be Turtle's parents. They "give" her to Taylor and express their wish for Taylor to adopt her. Note that as Esperanza tells her supposedly make-believe story, she goes through a catharsis, a purification that releases her bottled-up feelings about her real daughter, Ismene, and the atrocities that she has witnessed while living in Guatemala. By relating her personal story, Esperanza acknowledges that she no longer dreams of once again holding and caring for Ismene; she is saying good-bye to her daughter. Note, too, that she gives to Turtle her medal of St. Christopher, guardian saint of refugees, and then hands over Turtle to Taylor.

Because this scene in which Esperanza relinquishes her maternal rights of Ismene and her fictitious rights of Turtle is so sad and painful, Kingsolver interjects humor to lighten the tone. Taylor thinks that Esperanza plays her role as the sacrificing mother so well that she could win an Oscar nomination for best actress. Throughout the novel, Kingsolver injects such humor to lessen the emotionally weighty tone of the work.

When Taylor, Turtle, Estevan, and Esperanza finally leave Armistead's office, Taylor thinks of how the group is now a new community of friends and family. She realizes that Estevan and

Esperanza have sacrificed everything for her, including their pride, symbolized by their donning denim work clothes to make themselves look more poor than they really are.

In Chapter 17, Taylor safely delivers Estevan and Esperanza to a church that is part of the underground network known as the Sanctuary movement. Another difficult and emotional scene unfolds as they say good-bye to each other.

Taylor's calling her mother after leaving Estevan and Esperanza emphasizes the stabilizing role that her mother still plays in her life. Her mother is her refuge. Taylor feels proud as she tells her mother that she has adopted Turtle. When her mother uses a phrase that alludes to a child's legitimacy, Taylor chides her, but her mother reassures Taylor that children get their traits not only from their biological parents but from "what you tell them."

The other important phone call that Taylor makes is to 1-800-THE LORD. Rather naively, she wants to thank them for being there when she needed them, which is ironic given that she's never directly relied on them before. Taylor is incredulous when she discovers that the telephone number is not a help line at all, but a number to call to donate money. However, after she hangs up, she feels joy, for she now recognizes that she has survived the recent tough times with the help of her newfound family and friends, not with 1-800-THE LORD.

In the Oklahoma City public library, Taylor and Turtle look at a horticultural encyclopedia. Once again, Kingsolver's knowledge of natural history is evident. Taylor reads about the rhizobia, microscopic bugs that live on the roots of wisteria vines. Rhizobia perform a necessary role for wisteria vines: They produce fertilizer out of nitrogen gas. Here, Taylor makes a symbolic connection between the interdependence of the rhizobia and the wisteria plants and the interdependence among people. The relationship between the rhizobia and the wisteria symbolizes Taylor's positive, life-sustaining relationships with the many people she's met. Without this network of friends and family, she would not be the more mature, nurturing woman she's become.

Taylor now accepts the notion that she, Turtle, Lou Ann, and Dwayne Ray are a family. She explains to Turtle that Turtle is now, legally, Taylor's child, and then she calls Lou Ann to tell her that she and Turtle are on their way home. Lou Ann shares her good news that she has begun dating a new man—one she never would have had the courage to date before meeting Taylor—and has decided to reject Angel's offer to reconcile. But she assures Taylor that their family will remain intact. Lou Ann has grown more secure with herself and the decisions she makes, to a large degree because Taylor has empowered her to accept herself for who she is.

The novel ends with Taylor and Turtle heading back to Tucson, to their new home and family. The closing image is powerful in that Turtle acknowledges that they are going "home." Here, Turtle wholly accepts Taylor as her mother. To emphasize this point, Kingsolver has Turtle sing a song about vegetable soup that includes the names of people in her life, with Taylor as the "main ingredient." Kingsolver leaves very little doubt, if any, that Taylor will be a successful mother to Turtle, much like her own mother was to her. Note that the theme of going home here at the end of the novel balances the theme of departure at the beginning of the novel. Taylor has matured into a responsible woman who recognizes the interdependence of the varied people in her life.

- **Rastafarian**   a member of a Jamaican religion that awaits the redemption of Blacks and their return to Africa.

CRITICAL ESSAYS

KINGSOLVER'S STYLE

Barbara Kingsolver's style is poetic. She blends realism with lyricism, interspersed with humor, to create what critics have called a "southern novel taken west." Kingsolver accurately depicts the lives of common, everyday people (most of them women) by creating vivid images that provoke thoughts, feelings, and moods. For example, we hear the air gun as Taylor works on tires at Jesus Is Lord Used Tires, and we feel the same tingling in our fingers that Lou Ann feels after dicing hot chilies in a packing line at Red Hot Mama's salsa factory. Kingsolver describes the neighborhood where Taylor and Lou Ann live in Arizona as being "a little senile, with arthritic hinges and window screens hanging at embarrassing angles . . . transformed in ways that favored function over beauty." This image, which is both humorous and serious, gives readers a clear picture of Taylor's physical surroundings.

Kingsolver's native southern Kentucky dialect contributes to the realistic representation of the simple, ordinary life lived by her characters. Taylor and Lou Ann both grew up in rural Kentucky and consider themselves hillbillies. They feel comfortable with each other because they talk alike, using expressions such as "I'll swan" and "ugly as a mud stick fence."

Numerous examples of humor throughout the novel prevent the tone from becoming too serious and sad. For example, Lou Ann thinks that her cat has a split personality because "the good cat wakes up and thinks the bad cat has just pooped on the rug." And Taylor imagines Lou Ann going to a job interview and saying, "Really ma'am, I could understand why you wouldn't want to hire a dumb old thing such as myself." Kingsolver's abilities to relate life realistically with a sense of humor and to create detailed images from her perceptive observations enable her to invoke feelings of empathy for her characters and instill hope for a brighter future.

LITERARY TOOLS

Dialect. Kingsolver relies on her familiarity with Southern dialect to reinforce the realism and lyricism evident in her writing style. As a realist, she imitates what is real. The Southern dialect spoken by Taylor and Lou Ann is the dialect that Kingsolver remembers speaking while growing up in rural Kentucky. It is a dialect full of imagery that awakens the senses. Years after leaving Kentucky and her native dialect behind, Kingsolver utilized the poetic and unique features of that dialect to give her characters substance and personality.

A dialect is a spoken version of a language. Dialects develop when people are separated or isolated from one another due to natural geographic barriers, such as mountain ranges, or social barriers, such as class. Prior to the development of motorized travel, which allows people to move about more easily, and mass communication technology, including telephones, communication among regional groups of people was practically nonexistent. As a result, dialects are regional and often have distinct features of pronunciation, grammar, and vocabulary. There are three general areas in the United States in which people speak different dialects. The Eastern dialect is spoken in eastern New York and New England; the Southern dialect is spoken south of Pennsylvania and the Ohio River and westward beyond the Mississippi into Texas; and the rest of the country speaks what is called a General American or Western dialect.

The Southern dialect that Taylor, Lou Ann, and their relatives speak includes figurative language that creates images that tell stories about simple, daily occurrences. For example, when Taylor first meets Lou Ann, Lou Ann understands her perfectly when she says, "I'm just a plain hillbilly from East Jesus Nowhere with this adopted child that everybody keeps on telling me is dumb as a box of rocks. I've got nothing on you, girl." Other common expressions they use are "I'll swan," "ugly as a mud stick fence," and "everybody deserves their own piece of the pie." Taylor's mother uses expressions like "even a spotted pig looks black at night" and "that's my big girl bringing home the bacon." Lou Ann tells her mother and grandmother not to sit on a concrete bench because "it'll be hot as a poker in this sun."

When Estevan tells Taylor that the way she speaks is poetic, Taylor replies, "That's the biggest bunch of hogwash." Estevan tells her that "washing hogs is poetic." Because Estevan taught English in Guatemala, he is able to appreciate Taylor's colorful expressions.

The rural Kentucky dialect spoken by characters in *The Bean Trees* accurately depicts the dialect spoken in that particular region of the United States. Southern dialect is a tool that Kingsolver uses to realistically portray—at least to her—life lived by women from Kentucky.

Figurative Language. Kingsolver's lyricism transforms settings, scenes, characters, and actions into patterns of imagery, indirectly appealing to her readers' senses. The imagery in her prose is as vivid as the imagery found in poetry. Kingsolver makes use of figurative language—language that is taken figuratively as well as literally—to write a lyrical novel.

In *The Bean Trees*, figurative language includes metaphors and similes. Metaphors compare two unlike things without using words of comparison (*like* or *as*). In the novel, for example, when Taylor and Turtle are nearing Tucson, it begins to hail and the roads are covered with ice. Traffic is slow, and Kingsolver describes the pace as being "about the speed of a government check." Another example of Kingsolver's use of metaphor, this time influenced by her feminist views, is a humorous Valentine's Day card that Taylor buys for her mother. The card compares a man's helpfulness around the house to that of a pipe wrench. Kingsolver also relies on her extensive background in biology to include natural history metaphors. She compares the "thick, muscly [wisteria] vines" as they come out of the ground to "the arms of this guy who'd delivered Mattie's new refrigerator by himself."

Similes, comparisons of two unlike things that use words of comparison such as *like* or *as*, are direct comparisons that Kingsolver uses throughout the novel. At the beginning of the novel, Taylor relates how Newt Hardbine's daddy was thrown over the top of a Standard Oil sign "like some overalls slung over a fence"; she gives her new little Cherokee child the name Turtle because the girl is "like a mud turtle"; and later, while Taylor is getting her tires checked at Jesus Is Lord Used Tires, she watches as Mattie "rubbed Ivory soap on the treads and then dunked them in [a tub of water] like big doughnuts. Little threads of bubbles streamed up like strings of glass beads. Lots of them. It looked like a whole jewelry store in there."

Kingsolver's knowledge of biology is evident when she compares railroad tracks in Tucson to blood vessels in the human body. She writes that the tracks "at one time functioned as a kind of artery" and compares the once-busy railroad line to a blood vessel "carrying platelets to circulate through the [body's] lungs." Such figurative language, derived from Kingsolver's knowledge of biology, evokes vivid images throughout *The Bean Trees* and appeals indirectly to the reader's senses.

Allusion. Another figure of speech that Kingsolver often uses throughout *The Bean Trees* is allusion. She refers to historical or famous people, objects, and events to suggest more than what she is saying. Examples of Kingsolver's allusions include:

- Taylor's mother always told her that trading Foster, Taylor's father, for her "was the best deal this side of the Jackson Purchase."

- When Taylor was in high school, she had a new science teacher who "came high railing in there like some blond Paul McCartney."
- As Taylor and Turtle drive across the Arizona border, they see "clouds [that] were pink and fat and hilarious looking, like the hippo ballerinas in a Disney movie."
- Because Taylor is afraid that a tire will blow up whenever she goes to Jesus Is Lord Used Tires to check on her car, she "felt like John Wayne in that war movie where he buckles down his helmet, takes a swig of bourbon, and charges across the mine field yelling something like, 'Live Free or Bust!'"

Because the emotional effects created by allusions depend on the association that already exists in the reader's mind, it is necessary for the reader to either have knowledge of the allusions or be willing to research the allusions to understand the various meanings that Kingsolver attaches to them.

Symbolism. Symbols in *The Bean Trees* enrich the themes found in the novel and, oftentimes, suggest Kingsolver's extensive background in biology.

A symbol functions literally as a concrete object and figuratively as a representation of an idea. Symbols allow writers to compress complicated ideas or views into an image or word. Some symbols, such as a dove as a representation of peace or winter as a representation of death, are well known; they are called public symbols. Many times, writers invent their own symbols. When Kingsolver creates symbols, she has her own definite meanings for the symbols. However, because each symbol has a myriad of interpretations, she prefers that her readers interpret the symbolism as it relates to their own life experiences.

Much of the symbolism found in the novel is biological in nature, as Kingsolver repeatedly employs birds, plants, and animals. For example, the symbiotic relationship between the rhizobia and the wisteria vines represents the theme of the interdependency between people in a community. The "bean trees," or wisteria, that are able to thrive in non-fertile soil and the bird that builds its nest in a cactus ("You just couldn't imagine how she'd made a home in there") may symbolize the resiliency and ability to thrive that human beings (like Turtle) possess.

A bird is used as a symbol again later in the novel. After Turtle is molested in the park, a bird gets trapped in the house and, with Taylor's help, is freed. This trapped bird symbolizes the fact that Turtle is once again trapped within herself—she stops speaking and has a glazed look in her eyes—but with Taylor's help, Turtle is freed, too. This symbol reinforces the themes of interdependence between people, the importance of family, and hope for the future.

Fundamentalism as a *Leitmotif.* Fundamentalism is a religious movement that interprets scripture literally and applies it to daily life. Fundamentalism flourished during the twentieth century, particularly in the South. The doctrines of the movement were published around 1910 in pamphlets entitled *The Fundamentals.* Modern Fundamentalism stresses Bible study, is anti-intellectual, and is revivalist (involving highly emotional gatherings that serve to promote religion).

In literature or art, a *leitmotif* is an intentional repetition of an idea, word, phrase, or situation. Fundamentalism used as a *leitmotif* in *The Bean Trees* includes the Oral Roberts telephone number, 1-800-THE LORD. Taylor first sees the telephone number on an Oral Roberts television show (Roberts is a television evangelist) when she is in a restaurant in Oklahoma. The telephone number becomes a lifeline for Taylor, her "ace in the hole." She knows that if things get really bad, she can call 1-800-THE LORD to get help.

After Taylor "hit bottom and survived," she realizes that she no longer needs the security that having the telephone number gave her. She calls 1-800-THE LORD to thank them for the emotional and psychological support that they have given her—although, of course, they have no idea who Taylor is—and finds out that she's been deceived. The number is not a number to call for help, but a number to call to pledge money to Oral Roberts' ministry. Instead of being upset, Taylor asks them to give *her* a donation and is thankful that she is no longer in a position to need the number.

MAJOR THEMES IN THE NOVEL

Major themes in *The Bean Trees* include the importance of family and the need for community as emotional support systems for individuals facing hardships. Kingsolver uses her feminist beliefs, her interest in political issues, and her background in biology as vehicles to relate her thematic messages.

Throughout the novel, Kingsolver focuses on family as a major theme. Taylor ends up with Turtle, and together they form a family. When they move in with Lou Ann and her son, their family grows. Neither Taylor nor Lou Ann can afford much; by sharing expenses, they help each other survive difficult times. Lou Ann considers Taylor and Turtle family because they'd "been through hell and high water together" and because they know "each other's good and bad sides, stuff nobody else knows." Taylor and Lou Ann develop an enduring friendship and love for one another. Out of this sense of belonging and acceptance comes the notion of family, of unasked-for and freely given emotional and psychological support.

Other nontraditional families include Edna and Virgie Mae, as well as Mattie and her house full of political refugees. Because Edna is blind, she is dependent on Virgie Mae. They support and care for one another. Mattie, when asked if she has "grandbabies," responds, "Something like that." She loves the people who are in sanctuary in her house. They are fellow human beings, and she risks her life for them time and time again. What she does to care for and support these refugees is no different from what most biological family members do for each other.

Kingsolver's belief in community as a necessary support for individuals, as well as for American society, is another major theme. After Taylor and Turtle rent a room at the Hotel Republic and all of Taylor's money is spent, Taylor knows that she has to get a job; however, she finds herself in a situation too familiar to many single mothers: wondering how she will be able to afford childcare for Turtle. She feels guilty leaving Turtle at Kid Central Station in the mall and knows that she needs other resources. After Taylor moves in with Lou Ann, she finds a place where she belongs—a community, and resources within that community. She finds that she can depend on Lou Ann and her neighbors Edna and Virgie Mae to help care for Turtle. Even Mattie doesn't mind having Turtle in the Jesus Is Lord Used Tires shop while Taylor is working.

Estevan and Esperanza also become Taylor's friends and members of her community. They are people she depends on who also depend on her. Taylor takes a risk by driving them to Oklahoma to a safe house; in return, they risk their lives to save Turtle from becoming a ward of the state.

The willingness of people in a community to allow others to depend on them creates trust and a sense of belonging for both the providers and the receivers of that dependence. Community members look out for each other and support each other. In so doing, they allow all members to grow emotionally and to lead more productive lives without the worry of everyday personal security, including the need for food. Kingsolver portrays this interdependency between the community members symbolically in the symbiotic relationship between the wisteria vines and the rhizobia.

Exposing her readers to the value of community and family, Kingsolver's hope is to spur them to action, thereby making the world a kinder—and more secure—place in which to live.

KINGSOLVER'S WOMEN

The women in *The Bean Trees* portray feminist views shared by Kingsolver. They are strong, resilient women living in an imperfect world in late twentieth-century America. Their endurance, strong relationships, and commitment to their nontraditional families are paramount to their survival within the confines of society.

The women in the novel are ordinary, decent women. Their concerns, similar to those of most single women, include how to survive on very little income, how to keep their children clothed and fed, and how to keep a job and care for their children at the same time. Kingsolver considers these women heroes. They persevere in spite of the trials and tribulations they face, and discover resources in totally unexpected places.

Kingsolver's women survive with each other's help. The interdependent relationships that develop among them provide support and encouragement, enabling them to accomplish tasks that they could not accomplish alone. Esperanza is able to come to terms with the loss of Ismene when she has the opportunity to symbolically give up Turtle and say good-bye. If Taylor hadn't had Esperanza's support in return, she may have lost Turtle to the state. The relationships between the women, similar to the relationship between the rhizobia and the wisteria vines, are symbiotic because there is a steady give and take. As a result, like the wisteria vines, the women flourish.

All the women in the novel who have children are single mothers. Motherhood is the most important aspect of their lives. Taylor's mother worked as a housekeeper and raised Taylor alone. She always made it clear to Taylor that trading Taylor's father for her was "the best deal this side of the Jackson Purchase." Taylor, who was adamant about not wanting to be "barefoot and pregnant," willingly takes care of Turtle and loves her as though she is her natural-born child. Lou Ann, overprotective of her son, Dwayne Ray, does her best to be the perfect mother. Although these women have little to offer their children materially, they do offer them the things that count—love, a family, security, and stability. As Taylor tells Turtle, "You already know there's no such thing as promises. But I'll try as hard as I can to stay with you."

Because Kingsolver's women are, for the most part, single, men are not prominent characters in the novel. The attitude of the women toward men is not negative or antagonistic; it is indifferent. Taylor doesn't feel as though she suffered because she grew up without her father. In fact, as she grew up, she realized that there was more to life than facing a future "married to a tobacco farmer." Lou Ann's husband left her, and it didn't seem to matter that he wasn't around any longer. His presence had not been significant enough to miss. This prevailing attitude of the women toward men is expressed in the Valentine's Day card Taylor sends her mother. On the outside, the card reads, "Here's hoping you'll soon have something big and strong around the house to open those tight jar lids." On the inside is a picture of a pipe wrench.

The women quickly learn the benefits of knowing their neighbors and developing a community. Because American society is a mobile society, traditional communities, in which everyone knows and cares about everyone else, are disappearing. By creating a community for her women in the novel, Kingsolver is able to alert her readers to the importance of community and the contribution that it makes to the life of each and every member.

A NOTE ABOUT FEMINISM

Feminism is a philosophy advocating equal economic, political, and social rights and opportunities for women. The term has been used for close to a century in the United States: Even before winning the right to vote in 1920, women who sought women's rights called themselves feminists.

Between 1920 and 1960, enthusiasm for the women's rights movement decreased. The Equal Rights Amendment (ERA) to the United States Constitution, which would have made sex discrimination officially unconstitutional, caused feminists to split during the 1920s and form two camps—those who favored the ERA and those who opposed it. The Great Depression and World War II also hindered gains for feminists.

In the 1960s, political activism for women's rights began to increase. Two branches formed: a middle-aged group of professional women who advocated legislative reform, and a younger group of women who favored revolutionary change and called themselves women's liberationists. By the mid-1970s, these groups merged to form organizations such as the National Organization for Women (NOW).

During this time, President John F. Kennedy established a Presidential Commission on the Status of Women and, in 1961, named Eleanor Roosevelt its chairperson. The commission's report revealed widespread discrimination against women in the workplace, as well as in the law, and a lack of adequate childcare. In 1963, the first civil rights legislation for women, the Equal Pay Act, was passed. Since then, Congress has passed other laws prohibiting discrimination against women.

Through their writing, feminists such as Betty Friedan, Gloria Steinem, and Germaine Greer have brought awareness of the plight of women to the public. While attending college, Kingsolver read the writings of Friedan and Steinem. Greatly influenced by her readings, Kingsolver writes about women, their struggles to survive, their relationships with each other, and their commitment to motherhood.

In *The Bean Trees*, the protagonist and the other central characters are women. The women who have children (Taylor and Lou Ann) are either not married or separated from their husbands. They manage to survive by forming a community in which they can depend on each other. Throughout the novel, Kingsolver introduces feminist issues that she feels strongly about, such as childcare, sexual harassment, and the capabilities of women in typically male-dominated workplaces.

REVIEW QUESTIONS AND ESSAY TOPICS

(1) Analyze the "women's world" in which *The Bean Trees* takes place.

(2) How do the characters in *The Bean Trees* demonstrate that the role of women in America in the twentieth century has changed?

(3) List the social issues that Kingsolver presents in *The Bean Trees* and explain how these issues affect the lives of the novel's characters.

(4) Explain how the struggles faced by the characters in the novel are inspiring.

(5) How is Taylor Greer like Barbara Kingsolver?

(6) How are the people in Taylor's life interdependent?

(7) Why does Taylor participate in the Sanctuary movement?

(8) Compare the adventurous character of Taylor to the character of Lou Ann, who is terrified of life.

(9) Research the Cherokee Indian and Guatemalan peoples to learn more about the cultures Kingsolver refers to.

(10) Discuss the ways in which Taylor is a heroic character.

(11) One of the novel's themes is the importance of community. Why is community valued?

(12) How is the link between rhizobia (the microscopic bugs that live in the roots of legumes, turning nitrogen gas into fertilizer and allowing the plants to thrive in poor soil) and wisteria vines ("bean trees") similar to the relationships that form between the women in the novel?

(13) Kingsolver is a poet. Analyze selected passages of description as poetic prose, paying attention to such elements as metaphor, simile, and imagery.

(14) Compare the settings of Pittman County, Kentucky, and Tucson, Arizona, as Kingsolver describes them. How do these descriptions portray the moods of these places?

(15) How is language important in *The Bean Trees*?

KINGSOLVER'S PUBLISHED WORKS

The Bean Trees. New York: Harper & Row, 1988.
Holding the Line: Women in the Great Arizona Mine Strike of 1983 (nonfiction). New York: ILR Press, 1989.
Homeland and Other Stories. New York: HarperCollins, 1989.
Animal Dreams. New York: HarperCollins, 1990.
Another America/Otra America (poetry). California: Seal Press, 1992.
Pigs in Heaven. New York: HarperCollins, 1993.
High Tide in Tucson (essays). New York: HarperCollins, 1995.
The Poisonwood Bible. New York: HarperCollins, 1998.

SELECTED BIBLIOGRAPHY

"An Introduction to Barbara Kingsolver: A Brief Biography." HarperCollins. Internet. www.harpercollins.com. October 2, 1998.

"A Reader's Guide to the Fiction of Barbara Kingsolver: An Address from Barbara Kingsolver. Delivered at the 1993 American Booksellers Convention." HarperCollins. Internet. www.harpercollins.com. January 3, 1999.

"A Reader's Guide to the Fiction of Barbara Kingsolver: A Conversation with Barbara Kingsolver." HarperCollins. Internet. www.harpercollins.com. January 3, 1999.

"Barbara Kingsolver." HarperCollins. Internet. www.harper-collins.com. October 2, 1998.

"Barbara Kingsolver." Transcript of Interview with David Gergen, Editor of *U.S. News & World Report,* on November 24, 1995. Internet. www.usnews.com. January 23, 1999.

"Cherokee." *Microsoft Encarta 98 Encyclopedia.* CD-ROM. Microsoft Corporation: 1993-97.

"Civil Rights and Civil Liberties." *Microsoft Encarta 98 Encyclopedia.* CD-ROM. Microsoft Corporation: 1993-97.

Contemporary Authors New Revision Series. Vol. 60. Detroit: Gale Research, 1998. 206-208.

Contemporary Authors. Vol. 134. Detroit: Gale Research, 1992. 284-90.

Contemporary Literary Criticism Yearbook 1993. Vol. 81. Detroit: Gale Research, 1994. 190-95.

Contemporary Literary Criticism Yearbook 1988. Vol. 55. Detroit: Gale Research, 1989. 64-68.

Current Biography Yearbook 1994. New York: Wilson, 1995. 304-308.

EPSTEIN, ROBIN. "Barbara Kingsolver." *The Progressive.* Vol. 60, February 1996. 33.

FERRIS, ELIZABETH G. *The Central American Refugees.* New York: Praeger Publishers, 1987.

GOLDEN, RENNY, AND MICHAEL MCCONNELL. *Sanctuary: The New Underground Railroad.* New York: Orbis Books, 1986.

"LitChat: Barbara Kingsolver." *Salonmagazine.* Internet. www.sa-lon.com. August 26, 1998.

MCNEILL, MICHAEL. "La pasionaria: Barbara Kingsolver." *People Weekly.* October 11, 1993. 109.

RYAN, MAUREEN. "Barbara Kingsolver's Lowfat Fiction." *Journal of American Culture* (Winter 1995): 18, 77-81.

SEE, LISA. "Barbara Kingsolver: Her Fiction Features Ordinary People Heroically Committed to Political Issues." *Publisher's Weekly.* Vol. 237, August 31, 1990. 46.

"The Trail of Tears." North Georgia History. Internet. December 15, 1998.

"Women's Rights." *Microsoft Encarta 98 Encyclopedia.* CD-ROM. Microsoft Corporation: 1993-97.

WRIGHT, CHARLOTTE M. "Barbara Kingsolver." *Updating the Literary West.* Ft. Worth: Texas Christian University Press, 1997.